# Negotiating Against the Odds

# Negotiating Against the Odds

## A Guide for Trade Negotiators from Developing Countries

Emily Jones

*Deputy Director, Global Economic Governance Programme,*
*University of Oxford, UK*

First published 2013 by
PALGRAVE MACMILLAN

Palgrave Macmillan in the UK is an imprint of Macmillan Publishers Limited,
registered in England, company number 785998, of Houndmills, Basingstoke,
Hampshire RG21 6XS.

Palgrave Macmillan in the US is a division of St Martin's Press LLC,
175 Fifth Avenue, New York, NY 10010.

Palgrave Macmillan is the global academic imprint of the above companies
and has companies and representatives throughout the world.

Palgrave® and Macmillan® are registered trademarks in the United States,
the United Kingdom, Europe and other countries.

ISBN 978–1–137–32023–0

This book is printed on paper suitable for recycling and made from fully
managed and sustained forest sources. Logging, pulping and manufacturing
processes are expected to conform to the environmental regulations of the
country of origin.

A catalogue record for this book is available from the British Library.

A catalog record for this book is available from the Library of Congress.

10  9  8  7  6  5  4  3  2  1
22  21  20  19  18  17  16  15  14  13

# Contents

# Case Studies

# Acknowledgements

It has been a real privilege to author this guide, and while my name is on the cover, it is really the product of a whole team of people, including more than one hundred experienced trade negotiators, diplomats, politicians, policy experts and academics who generously shared their insights and experiences along the way.

The guide is the result of a long-standing collaboration between the Global Economic Governance Programme at the University of Oxford and the Commonwealth Secretariat. I would like to thank Edwin Laurent, who first conceived of this guide; Edwin Laurent and Ngaire Woods for overseeing and guiding the project at every step and making numerous thoughtful contributions; Tyler Mattiace and Tasneem Clarke for excellent research assistance; Taylor St John for helpful comments and editing; James Lees for assisting with the index and Reija Fanous, Shaneez Hassan and Esther Amon for invaluable administrative assistance. On the publishing side, I am grateful for the support of Sherry Dixon at the Commonwealth Secretariat, and Christina Brian and Amanda McGrath at Palgrave Macmillan. In addition, I would like to thank the Commonwealth Secretariat for financing the research process.

I am particularly indebted to the following people for having contributed substantively to the early drafts of this work, through workshops, interviews and written comments: Ahmed Aslam, Assad Bhuglah, Carolyn Deere Birkbeck, Elizabeth Tuerk, John Odell, Kathy-Ann Brown, Keith Nurse, Lingston Cumberbatch, Marwa Kisiri, Michanne Haynes Prempeh, Mohammed Irfan, Mohammad Razzaque, Morgan Githinji, Nimrod Waniala, Ousseni Illy, Roman Grynberg, Ronald Sanders, Samual Passow, Sheila Page, Teddy Soobramanien, Vaughan Lewis, Veniana Qalo and Victor Kitange. While I have done my utmost to ensure that their thoughts and experiences are accurately reflected, any errors or omissions remain very much my own.

# Acronyms

| | |
|---|---|
| ACP | African, Caribbean and Pacific |
| AGOA | African Growth and Opportunity Act |
| BATNA | Best alternative to a negotiated agreement |
| BIT | Bilateral investment treaty |
| C4 | Cotton Four (Benin, Burkina Faso, Mali and Chad) |
| CARICOM | Caribbean Community |
| CRNM | Caribbean Regional Negotiating Machinery |
| DR-CAFTA | Dominican Republic Central America Free Trade Agreement |
| DSM (WTO) | Dispute Settlement Mechanism |
| ECDPM | European Centre for Development Policy Management |
| ECLAC | Economic Commission for Latin America and the Caribbean |
| ECOWAS | Economic Commission for West African States |
| EPA | Economic Partnership Agreement |
| EPZ | Export processing zone |
| EU | European Union |
| FDI | Foreign direct investment |
| FTA | Free Trade Agreement |
| G20 | Group of 20 |
| G33 | Group of 22 |
| G90 | Group of 90 |
| GATS | General Agreement on Trade in Services |
| GATT | General Agreement on Tariffs and Trade |
| ICC | International Chamber of Commerce |
| ICSID | International Centre for Settlement of Investment Disputes |
| ICT | Information and Communication Technology |
| ICTSD | International Centre for Trade and Sustainable Development |
| IISD | International Institute for Sustainable Development |
| ILEAP | International Lawyers and Economists Against Poverty |
| JEC (Mauritius) | Joint Economic Council |

| | |
|---|---|
| LDC | Least developed country |
| LDC Group | Least Developed Countries Group (at the WTO) |
| LMG | Like-Minded Group (of States at the WTO) |
| ODI | Overseas Development Institute |
| OECD | Organisation of Economic Co-operation and Development |
| OECS | Organisation of Eastern Caribbean States |
| NAFTA | North American Free Trade Agreement |
| NGO | Non-governmental organisation |
| PIFS | Pacific Islands Forum Secretariat |
| PLN | Partido Liberación Nacional |
| TMNP | Temporary migration of natural persons |
| TRALAC | Trade Law Centre |
| TRIPS | Trade-Related Aspects of Intellectual Property Rights |
| UN | United Nations |
| UNCTAD | United Nations Conference on Trade and Development |
| UNECA | United Nations Economic Commission for Africa |
| UPU | Universal Postal Union |
| WCO | World Customs Organization |
| WTO | World Trade Organization |
| ZOPA | Zone of possible agreement |

# 1
# Introduction

How do you succeed in a negotiation with a far larger party? Negotiators from many developing countries face this challenge on a regular basis. Asymmetries are most obvious when small developing countries negotiate with large industrialised countries or blocs such as the United States or European Union or with large developing countries such as China or Brazil. However, they are often present when they negotiate with larger neighbouring countries, or with multinational companies.

Negotiations in international trade are important for many developing countries. Many have small domestic markets, so trade with other countries is vital, and their high reliance on international trade makes them particularly vulnerable to changes in the rules that govern it. As a result, they have a strong interest in the outcomes of international trade negotiations.

Yet, when it comes to shaping these rules, these countries face many well-known structural, economic and political constraints. Due to their small market size, they have little to offer negotiating partners by way of market access concessions, the major currency of trade negotiations. Their institutional capacity is often limited so they have few trade negotiators and limited budgets. Compounding this, they may feel under pressure from more powerful states to comply with their interests.

Given these constraints, can negotiators from developing countries really expect to influence the outcome when they negotiate with a far larger party? While negotiators from smaller countries might not be able to 'win' every time, some do better than others. Experiences shows us that a smaller party can augment its power through the skilful use of negotiating strategies and tactics. Time and again, the smaller party proves that it is more powerful than it appears at first glance, and the larger party turns out to be weaker than it first assumes. As a result, 'the less powerful party in an international negotiation is not necessarily at the mercy of a more powerful party' (Salacuse 2000: 257).

> *The less powerful party in an international negotiation is not necessarily at the mercy of a more powerful party.*

## Aim of this guide

This guide explores the ways in which developing countries can influence outcomes when they negotiate with larger parties. It was written in response to requests from negotiators, who wanted a resource that brought together practical advice and lessons in an accessible manner. It sets out to answer the question, 'How can negotiators from small developing countries maximise their leverage and influence in international negotiations?'

It will be useful for those who are, or expect to be, engaged in negotiating on behalf of most developing countries, including officials of national governments, as well as advisers based in regional and international organisations. It will also be valuable for parliamentarians and representatives of private sector and civil society organisations, whether they are directly involved in negotiations or seek to influence the outcomes from outside. Finally, it will be useful for journalists and researchers, who seek to understand negotiating processes and explain their outcomes to the wider public.

While it focuses on international trade, the advice and many of the lessons contained in this guide are relevant to other areas of international negotiation, including aid, climate change and financial regulation.

The guide adopts no formal definition of a 'small developing country'. Negotiators consulted during the production of the guide felt that the advice and lessons are likely to be useful to the majority of developing countries. With the exception of the very largest, developing countries frequently negotiate under conditions of asymmetry, interacting with parties that are far larger and better resourced.

## Can negotiating really make a difference?

The manifold problems that negotiators from small developing countries face can lead to the pessimistic view that 'no amount of negotiating will make a difference'. Evidence from surveys and interviews suggests that many negotiators have low expectations of success in negotiations with larger countries. In a survey of negotiators from small developing countries, conducted by the author more than half of the 93 respondents expected to have 'low influence' over the outcomes, while a fifth expected to have 'no influence' at all. Yet, more revealingly, interviews suggest that when negotiators from small developing countries have low expectations of success, they do not use leverage that they do have to the fullest extent. In the words of one negotiator, 'we are not trying to influence negotiations. It's unrealistic so we don't go in with that mindset' (Jones et al. 2010: 63).

While it is important not to underestimate the constraints small developing countries face, the examples and experiences in this guide provide cause for optimism. Through effective negotiation, small developing countries can avoid entering into agreements that they should reject, and they can successfully influence outcomes and obtain meaningful concessions. As another negotiator notes, 'when you are small, you need to find other angles and approaches. Get yourself around the wall, don't try and go over it. Meeting a wall doesn't necessarily mean your objective cannot be reached' (Jones et al. 2010: 54).

*Get yourself around the wall, don't try and go over it. Meeting a wall doesn't necessarily mean your objective cannot be reached.*

## Sources and structure

This guide brings together valuable insights on ways to negotiate effectively and to avoid common pitfalls. It draws on three principal sources of information:

- The experiences of more than 100 negotiators from small developing countries, gathered through an online survey, in-depth interviews, focus-group discussions and detailed case studies (these are analysed in detail in Jones et al. 2010).
- An extensive review of the literature on negotiations, including from the business world and studies by scholars of international relations.
- The findings and lessons were 'road-tested' by a group of leading negotiators from small developing countries.

It examines a broad range of international trade negotiations in which there is a substantial difference in the size of the parties at the negotiating table. This includes multilateral negotiations under the auspices of the World Trade Organization; regional integration projects between neighbouring countries of differing sizes; and bilateral negotiations including on free trade agreements and bilateral investment treaties. The guide also draws examples from negotiations between host governments and foreign investors. Although there are important differences between government-investor and inter-governmental negotiations, negotiations with private parties offer useful lessons for other asymmetric negotiations. In addition, negotiating well with foreign investors is a crucial part of surviving and thriving in the global economy.

Five chapters follow this Introduction:

- **Chapter 2: Preparation and Diagnosis.** Accurately diagnosing the situation is essential for negotiating effectively. This chapter highlights key aspects of preparation and diagnosis, including convening the best possible negotiating team; identifying your country's own interests and negotiating objectives, as well as those of other parties; the importance of establishing alternatives and thinking creatively about sources of leverage and influence; and developing a clear negotiating mandate.

- **Chapter 3: Moves Away from the Negotiating Table.** Many of the important decisions that affect outcomes are taken either before the parties sit down at the table or away from the table once negotiations are underway. This chapter includes selecting the right forum and issues for discussion, creating coalitions and alliances, ensuring that the best people are at the table, and taking steps to influence public opinion. While much of the focus is on interaction with the representatives of the other party, actively managing relations with constituencies outside of the negotiating room is crucially important.

- **Chapter 4: Moves at the Negotiating Table.** Once at the negotiating table, it is important to select appropriate tactics: framing your case persuasively, neutralising pressure tactics, and using personal behaviours and attributes to best effect. Three lessons, in particular, stand out. The first is the importance of psychology; to maximise their leverage, negotiators from small developing countries need to be optimistic, creative and tenacious. The second is the need to be thorough and vigilant, particularly with regard to scrutinising information and the moves of the other party. The third is the need to adapt, modifying your strategy and tactics in response to the moves of the other parties and changes in the environment outside the negotiating room.

- **Chapter 5: Putting the Right Foundations in Place.** To maximise leverage in a given negotiation, it is vital that a series of underlying factors are addressed. This chapter covers recruiting and retaining high-calibre officials, ensuring smooth inter-governmental communication, strengthening coalitions and regional organisations, managing and improving input from interest groups and strengthening the evidence base.
- **Chapter 6: Conclusion.** The guide concludes by reflecting on four overarching lessons that emerge from the preceding chapters, and suggests further reading.

A key lesson, and one that the guide emphasises throughout, is that small developing countries need to involve a wide range of policy- and decision-makers in order to maximise their influence in trade negotiations. This includes senior government officials and politicians, and, in some cases, parliamentarians, and representatives of business and civil society. Accordingly, the guide uses the term 'negotiator' in a flexible manner, often referring to all those who have a significant role to play in policy- and decision-making during negotiations, irrespective of whether or not they sit at the negotiating table.

# 2
# Preparation and Diagnosis

If there is one lesson that emerges from the negotiation literature, it is the importance of thorough preparation. Inadequate preparation is one of the most common and costly mistakes in negotiations, and the investment needed should not be underestimated (Malhotra and Bazerman 2007). As an experienced negotiator notes, 'Planning in negotiation is as meticulous as preparation for war' and it can involve weeks of arduous work (Bhuglah 2004). As a rule of thumb, one expert suggests that 80 per cent of the work in a given negotiation should go into preparation, and 20 per cent into the negotiation itself (Thompson 2012).

*Planning in negotiation is as meticulous as preparation for war and it can involve weeks of arduous work.*

Two types of preparation are important in a trade negotiation. The first concerns the steps that need to be taken before entering into a specific negotiation. This includes accurately diagnosing the situation, convening the best possible negotiating team identifying precise negotiating objectives and developing a clear negotiating mandate. These are addressed in this chapter.

The second type of preparation is longer term. Long-term preparation focuses on improving the underlying institutions in order to bolster a country's overall negotiating capacity. Key improvements include recruiting and retaining high-calibre negotiators, developing a strong evidence base, strengthening cross-government coordination and finding ways to effectively solicit contributions from stakeholders. These are addressed in Chapter 5.

## Types of negotiation

In our increasingly complex, diverse and dynamic world, negotiation is one of the most practical and effective mechanisms we have for allocating resources, balancing competing interests and resolving conflicts of all kinds (Malhotra and Bazerman 2007). This is true for trade, as it is for many other areas of international life.

A key condition for negotiation is that there must be a degree of interdependence between the parties. Independent parties do not negotiate because they do not need the other party to achieve their goals. At the other extreme, in situations of complete dependency, no negotiation is needed as the stronger party can dominate its counterpart and take whatever it wants.

Many people see a negotiation as a battle line, in which one side's gain necessarily implies another side's loss: Parties sit down at the bargaining table with the sole objective of walking away with their share and most of the other party's too. While it is possible to conceive of purely 'win-lose' or 'zero-sum' negotiations, much of the literature on negotiations is dedicated to debunking this myth, and showing that in most negotiations it is possible for the parties to work together to *create new value*, resulting in an agreement that can, in principle, leave everyone better off.

However, this does not mean that most negotiations are purely 'win-win', cooperative affairs. Indeed, far from it. In a typical negotiation, negotiators have two objectives. They seek to *create* as much joint value as possible (thereby maximising the size of the pie) and to *claim* as much value as possible for their party (thereby maximising the size of their slice). Such negotiations are referred to as 'variable-sum'.

---

**Three types of negotiation**

- *'Win-lose'*, where interests are diametrically opposed so a 'win' for one party is a 'loss' for the other, and the only incentive of the parties is to compete;

- *'Win-win'*, where the interests of the parties are entirely complementary and the only incentive of the parties is to cooperate;

- *'Variable-sum'*, where the parties have incentives both to cooperate in order to realise joint gains and to compete over division of resources that are generated in order to maximise their share.

---

'Variable-sum' negotiations pose a challenge for negotiators as they have incentives to both cooperate (to realise joint gains) and to compete (over the division of these gains). Managing the tension between these two incentives requires significant skill. Hardball moves to claim value can result in a loss of trust and cooperation, leading to unnecessary impasse and breakdown. Yet being too open and trusting can lead to the more cooperative party walking away with little of the value that it helped to create (Lax and Sebenius 2006; Thompson 2012). Techniques for overcoming the 'negotiator's dilemma' are discussed in Chapter 4.

In the trade context, most negotiations are 'variable-sum'. Indeed, recent survey evidence suggests that negotiators from small developing countries typically see negotiations with large countries as 'variable-sum' rather than the extremes of 'win-win' or 'win-lose'. In a survey negotiators were asked 'how often are the outcomes that your country is seeking in trade negotiations compatible with those of powerful states?' Of the 93 respondents, drawn from 30 small developing countries, 8 answered 'nearly always' or 'often', 45 answered 'sometimes', and 40 answered 'seldom' or 'almost never' (Jones et al. 2010: 83).

During a 'variable-sum' negotiation, studies show that it is common for negotiators to focus their attention on the 'win-lose' aspects, overlooking the potential areas for joint gain. Negotiators focusing on the 'win-lose' aspects usually adopt one of three mindsets when preparing for negotiation. They resign themselves to capitulation (common among weaker parties); prepare themselves for attack (common among the stronger parties); or seek to compromise in an attempt to split the value on the table. These mindsets run the risk of an inefficient negotiation where value is left 'on the table' (Thompson 2012).

Discussions with negotiators from small developing countries suggest that they do not always accurately diagnose the negotiation. In some instances, they wrongly assume that their interests are diametrically opposed to those of large states and that there is no possibility for joint gain. This possibility is particularly likely if there has been animosity between the two parties in the past. In other instances, negotiators wrongly assume that the large country will be flexible. This may arise because the other party has a long history of being a major aid donor, so the developing country expects it to adopt a benevolent approach. Alternatively, the smaller country may expect the larger to be flexible because it considers itself to be an important political ally. Colombia, for instance, mistakenly assumed that the United States would be generous in trade negotiations because it perceived itself to be a strategic ally (Garay et al. 2011).

A further common pitfall is that negotiators fail to identify the best moment for meaningful negotiation. In international trade negotiations, key decisions are often made by large states far in advance of the formal negotiations. For instance, the United States and the European Union (EU) develop detailed negotiating mandates as well as template legal texts before bilateral negotiations. These 'model' free trade agreements (FTAs) or bilateral investment treaties are often the product of intense internal political debate. When formal negotiations start, a model text is often presented to developing countries as 'fait accomplis', and there is often little room for influence, except at the margins. In some instances, including in the case of the EU and the United States, negotiators tie their hands by having the model text approved by senior ministers or the legislature, to whom they have to revert for approval in order to make even minor changes. In such situations, developing countries are likely to have greater impact over the final outcome if they can influence these up-stream processes, by developing alliances with political stakeholders in the large states who can push for greater flexibility when the negotiating mandate or template text is first drafted.

*All too often small developing countries undermine their influence by failing to participate actively in the initial deliberations.*

Similarly, while large ministerial meetings and summits capture the headlines, leaders often meet at such occasions to endorse agreements that have been hammered out by senior officials during preparatory talks. All too often small developing countries undermine their influence by failing to participate actively in the initial deliberations, focusing their resources on attending the high-profile meetings instead. For instance, during the 2011 UNCTAD (United Nations Conference on Trade and Development) IV Conference for Least Developed Countries, several least developed countries sent large, high-level delegations in the hope that this would enable them to secure concessions from industrialised countries. However, they came away with very little as the major decisions had all been made beforehand and many of the major industrialised countries were not even represented at a senior level during the meeting.

## Success in a negotiation

What counts as success in a negotiation? The negotiating literature has a variety of different definitions. The following is one of the more helpful:

> The negotiating objective should be to create and claim value for the long term by crafting and implementing a deal that is satisfactory for both (or all) parties.
>
> (Lax and Sebenius 2006: 16)

At the heart of this definition is the need for an effective negotiator to fulfil the twin objectives of creating and claiming value: helping create as much joint value as is possible so that nothing is 'left on the table', and claiming as much of this value as possible for their own party.

Three other features of this definition are worth noting. First, success in a negotiation is subjective, and depends on how each party perceives its interests, rather than being evaluated against some externally generated 'objective criteria'. In other words, a negotiation is successful if the parties involved deem it to be so. Second, and related, the definition highlights the importance of considering whether the other party is satisfied with the outcome. This is not only for altruistic reasons. If the other party feels that it has been treated unfairly or is unhappy with the outcome for another reason, they are likely to find ways to renege on their commitments and avoid implementation. Third, the definition refers to the 'long term'. In many negotiations, particularly in international affairs, a trade negotiation is only one fragment of a much broader and longer-term relationship between countries. Any evaluation of success needs to take into account the impact of a negotiation on this long-term relationship, as well as on the country's wider reputation: excessive hard bargaining might lead to a larger slice of the pie, but it might also damage your relationship and ruin your reputation (Malhotra and Bazerman 2007).

*What does success look like in a trade context?* Discussions with negotiators suggest the need to differentiate between three levels of success.

The first level of success is the ability to influence the negotiating process. A small state may successfully manoeuvre in a negotiation and have a decisive impact on the process, such as managing to propel its issue or concerns to the top of the negotiating agenda, or reframing the debate in its favour. For instance, the four cotton-exporting West African countries were successful in making cotton subsidies one of the most talked-about aspects of the Doha Round (Case Study 20). Similarly, through the creative use of media stunts, the president of the Maldives became a leading figure in climate change negotiations (Case Study 15). However, as with these examples, influencing the process does not always translate into influence over outcomes.

---

**Three levels of success in a negotiation**

Level 1: Influencing the negotiating process;

Level 2: Securing a negotiated outcome that reflects offensive and defensive interests (including walking away from a bad deal);

Level 3: Ensuring any gains are secured and losses are avoided during implementation.

---

The second, more substantive level of success is the ability to influence the final outcome of the negotiation. This is measured in terms of the degree to which the outcome furthers a country's offensive interests or protects its defensive interests. As with the definition of success cited above, perceptions of interests differ, so it is usually most appropriate to measure success against what a country perceives its interests to be, rather than against some external 'objective' criterion. In practical terms, this means measuring the outcome against the objectives that were set for the negotiators at the start, usually documented in the country's negotiating mandate. However, as the process of defining national negotiating objectives is often contested, even if negotiators are successful in meeting their negotiating objectives, interest groups or citizens in that country may dispute the outcome and argue that the negotiating objectives did not reflect their country's true interests.

When evaluating the outcome, it is important to measure success against the likely counterfactuals – the alternative outcomes that could have happened. In particular, it is key to recognise that in some situations *not* reaching agreement may be a relatively successful outcome. 'No agreement' might be considered a success if a country has avoided entering into an agreement that entailed making concessions in areas that are of vital defensive interest. As discussed below, an important skill for a negotiator is to know when it is in their country's interests not to reach an agreement.

*In some situations not reaching agreement may be a relatively successful outcome.*

The third level on which to measure success is during implementation. Ultimately, success in negotiation is the ability to not only secure an outcome on paper but also ensure that this leads to tangible gains in practice. For instance, a country may secure market access commitments in the services sector, only to find difficulties in concluding the mutual recognition agreements that are needed to turn this gain into a real advantage. Or it may negotiate for preferential market access for a particular product, only to find that its exporters are unable to meet the product standards of that market.

In many cases, the negotiating process does not end when a text is signed. Developing countries can be frustrated that even when they manage to obtain significant concessions from larger states during a negotiation, the latter sometimes renege upon their commitments during implementation. In other cases, developing countries obtain important concessions in the negotiating room, but a variety of political and economic pressures outside of the negotiating room may prevent them from using them in practice (see Deere Birkbeck 2009 for a fascinating account of the implementation of the Trade-Related Aspects of Intellectual Property Rights (TRIPS) Agreement).

Developing countries can also use the implementation period to their advantage, particularly if they have made costly concessions during a negotiation, as they may be able to find ways to avoid or delay making concessions in practice. In such situations, there may be advantages to being small, as larger countries may invest less in monitoring and enforcement, making it easier to 'fly under the radar'.

## Create (and retain) the best possible negotiating team

Selecting the best possible negotiating team is one of the first vital steps that a country can take in its bid to influence an upcoming negotiation. If this is done at the earliest stages of the process, then the team can work together to undertake the diagnostic and preparatory work outlined in the remainder of this chapter, which helps ensure that the whole team is thoroughly prepared before negotiations start in earnest. It enables the team to understand precisely what it is negotiating for and why; to develop effective ways of working; and to forge a collective team spirit.

Given the constraints of a relatively small human resource base and limited financial resources, what factors should be considered when creating the best possible negotiating team? The attributes and qualities of the team members are of paramount importance, and negotiators emphasise that quality is often more important than quantity. When asked in a survey and interviews to identify the most important personal qualities of negotiators, representatives from small developing countries emphasised the need for 'experience in trade negotiations', 'technical knowledge' and 'strategic thinking'. These were ranked as being more important than qualities such as charisma and linguistic skills that are often associated with good diplomacy. As one negotiator noted,

> [Y]ou don't need the kind of good diplomat who knows how to distinguish between malt whisky and blended whisky. You need someone who can understand the difference between a tariff, a specific duty, and an ad valorem duty.
>
> (Jones et al. 2010: 23)

---

**What makes a good negotiator?**

- Negotiating expertise;
- Technical knowledge;
- Strategic/political thinking;
- Tenacity and determination;
- Endurance/physical fitness;
- High levels of confidence and self-esteem.

---

When thinking about the qualities of a good negotiator, it is helpful to distinguish between 'experience' and 'expertise'. Experience is gained from engaging in a particular behaviour (such as negotiation) many times. Expertise is gained by when a negotiator is able to infuse this experience with what one book describes as a 'strategic conceptualisation' of what they are doing (Malhotra and Bazerman 2007). Thus, while a government official may have participated in many negotiations, and have a great deal of experience, they are not necessarily an expert negotiator: expertise comes from combining experience with analytical insights.

Tenacity, endurance, physical fitness and confidence are additional qualities that are particularly important for negotiators from small delegations, and are often overlooked. Trade negotiations are intense, and can run through the night, often for several days at a time.

While some countries have a large enough delegation to operate a shift system and bring in rested negotiators at frequent intervals, this option is rarely available for small countries. In such circumstances, determination and the physical fitness to persevere are distinct assets. Moreover, as discussed in later chapters, large states often use tactics that rely on making negotiators from smaller states feel inferior, in terms of the expertise or knowledge at their disposal, which makes high levels of confidence and self-esteem invaluable attributes.

These findings reinforce the lessons from other parts of this guide: a sound grasp of the technical details enables countries to manoeuvre wisely in the negotiating room, while strategic thinking enables them to make maximum use of their sources of power and influence outside of the negotiating room. They also underscore the importance of developing countries retaining experts in their civil service, a challenge that is examined in depth in Chapter 5.

Broadly speaking, a negotiating team needs to fulfil four key roles, each requiring different skills and often requiring more than one person:

- The 'lead negotiator' heads the team and speaks on its behalf, and should have a sound grasp of the technical details, a high level of diplomatic and negotiating expertise, excellent interpersonal skills, as well as an appropriate level of political authority. In instances of complex negotiations of long duration, countries usually have a deputy lead negotiator who can provide support and step in if the lead negotiator leaves.
- The 'technical experts' need to have specialised legal and economical knowledge in each of the issues on the table. There is usually at least one technical expert for each area of specialisation. In complex negotiations, there is often a lead specialist who negotiates the technical details in a particular issue-area on the table. They are supported by a team of researchers and advisers working in the 'back-room', often based in the capital.
- The 'political strategists' ensure that the team is using all its sources of potential influence to maximum effect. The strategists need to have an astute understanding of tactical negotiating moves, and deep political knowledge about the other party and as well as politics at home, and be effective listeners.
- Finally, the 'record keepers' document the proceedings both for future planning and for reporting back to constituencies.

---

**Putting together a negotiating team**

What technical expertise is required, and is this adequately represented on our team? Legal? Economic? Industry specific?

Do we have seasoned diplomats and negotiators? Do we have people with intimate knowledge of the domestic politics; key commercial interests; and political institutions of the other side?

Who should lead the delegation? At what political level should we be represented? What signal will this send our negotiating partners?

If private sector and civil society members are included, are they representative of broad stakeholder groups, or specific industries? If the latter, have we taken steps to mitigate the risks of capture?

---

The competence of the lead negotiator is an important consideration: how prepared they are, how well they argue their case and their grasp of the technical details. In addition, it is helpful to consider the signal that their political status sends to the other negotiating parties. For instance, sending a high-status representative to meet a low-status representative from the other side can lower leverage and influence, particularly when interpreted by the other side as a sign of desperation for an agreement. Conversely, if a relatively junior official is appointed as lead, the other party may interpret it as a sign that the negotiation is not being taken seriously.

It is vital that the briefing given to the lead negotiator is of high quality. Seasoned negotiators point out that developed countries are often more successful in the ministerial meetings of the World Trade Organization (WTO) not because their ministers have a better grasp of the technical details but because they are better briefed: They are given clear instructions on what to achieve, the key arguments to make and on the strategies and tactics to employ and to anticipate from the other parties. In contrast, ministers from developing countries often find themselves poorly briefed, with a mass of detailed information that is hard to digest, and without a clear sense of what they are aiming for, or the strategy they should pursue.

Although some negotiations, such as the negotiation of bilateral investment treaties, are over in a matter of weeks, other negotiations, including the negotiation of FTAs, often take many years. For this reason, retaining the core members of the team throughout a negotiation is important for ensuring success. When embarking on such negotiations, it is helpful to think through ways to keep key negotiators in place. This is discussed further in Chapter 5.

*Developed countries are often more successful not because they have higher-quality ministers, but because their ministers are better briefed.*

Given the shortage of government officials in many developing countries, it is common for some negotiators to be drawn from the private sector, academia and, in some cases, from civil society. There are two competing factors to weigh when deciding how to involve non-state actors, particularly from the private sector, in the negotiating team: information and accountability. Industry representatives can bring invaluable specialised knowledge of their industry. However, negotiators caution that when industry representatives are in the room, it can be harder to make a concession that is in the national interest if that damages the particular sector from which the representative is drawn. Moreover, since the industry representative often has more information and expertise than the government, they may be able to wield undue influence over the government's negotiating position.[1]

To mitigate these risks, it may be advisable to only invite industry representatives to be present for limited parts of the negotiation, or to have them in the 'room next door' so that they can be consulted readily and frequently as the negotiation progresses. An alternative option is to draw private sector representatives from broad umbrella organisations such as the chamber of commerce, but this runs the risk that they will have a lower level of specialist knowledge. In the longer term, it is advisable that governments develop their own technical expertise in key export sectors to reduce the information asymmetry between government and industry. Mauritius, Mexico and Nicaragua provide examples of these different approaches (Case Study 1).

### Case Study 1: Expertise and accountability tensions: involving the private sector in negotiations

*Direct Participation: Mauritius*

In Mauritius, the policy-making process is characterised by strong cross-sector cooperation within the private sector and a close partnership between the private sector and government, and trade negotiations are no exception. The Joint Economic Council (JEC), the apex body representing the private sector, brings together leading industry organisations and wields considerable influence over public policy, especially in the area of international trade. During negotiations, the JEC has an 'interactive' relationship with government, sharing information and resources, collaborating on research and contributing to trade missions and negotiations. In recent years, almost half of the core negotiating team has been drawn from the private sector and includes representatives of apex organisations like the JEC as well as industry representatives from sugar and banking.

This close collaboration has helped Mauritius gain its reputation for strong and effective negotiating. However, there are concerns that the perspectives of smaller industries and other stakeholders, including labour unions, are not well reflected.

### The 'Room Next Door' Model: Mexico and Nicaragua

In a number of countries, the private sector and other stakeholders participate in trade negotiations through the 'room next door' model. During the NAFTA (North American Free Trade Agreement) negotiations, for example, Mexico brought representatives from its private sector apex organisation to the location of the negotiations, and they stayed in a room close by, if not on site, and discussed the Mexican position with the negotiating team before and after each day of negotiations. Similarly, during the DR-CAFTA (Dominican Republic Central America Free Trade Agreement) negotiations, Nicaragua brought representatives from both the private sector and civil society to the negotiations and kept them close by where they could have 'constant access to each other's inputs throughout the negotiations'.

Having private sector representatives close at hand enabled negotiators to obtain direct information on the offensive and defensive interests of their industries, which proved invaluable as the negotiations evolved. However, the 'room next door' model has drawn criticism from some for often excluding small businesses not represented by apex organisations, as well as labour and civil society, while increasing the voice of those already participating in the policy process.

*Sources*: Alba and Vega (2002), Carrion (2009) and Jones et al. (2010).

## Know your interests

Perhaps the most fundamental step in preparing for an international trade negotiation is to know what you are seeking to obtain. Only once a country has identified its key interests, it can resolutely pursue them and decide where to concentrate its energies. As one expert advises: 'Choose your battles. Be targeted, focused and clinical. Find the niches to exploit.'[2]

This is particularly important for small teams of negotiators, who can become overwhelmed by the sheer number of negotiations they are involved in, as well as the number of issues at the table. For instance, in recent years, the majority of African countries, often with only a handful of officials working on trade negotiations, have been involved simultaneously in the Doha Round of negotiations at the WTO, in Economic Partnership Agreement (EPA) negotiations with the EU, in regional integration negotiations with their neighbours and with a series of bilateral investment treaties.

Yet interviews reveal that representatives from developing countries often enter negotiations without a clear understanding of their country's interests or clear directives setting out how they should try to further these interests in that particular negotiation. Without clear direction, it is extremely difficult for negotiators to succeed. Negotiators either use their own judgement to determine a negotiating agenda or they merely react to agendas and issues pursued by other states. As one negotiator observed, 'Our biggest problem is within our government. It is our inability to decide what our trade policy is. There is a total absence of trade policy' (Jones et al. 2010: 36).

> *Without clear direction from capital, it is extremely difficult for negotiators to succeed.*

Before entering a negotiation, negotiators need to establish the *best possible* outcome that their country could obtain, referred to in the negotiating literature as the 'target' or 'aspiration' point (Fisher and Ury

1991; Malhotra and Bazerman 2007). This requires a detailed understanding of their country's objectives in trade (both offensive and defensive) and the extent to which the particular negotiation could further them. For instance, a country's primary offensive objective may be to expand market access for its apparel exports. Analysis might suggest that exports are impeded by complex rules of origin and higher margins of preference being given to competitors. In this case, the 'target' or 'aspiration point' for negotiators might be to obtain the same tariff level as key competitors, together with simplified rules of origin.

A clear aspiration point serves as an invaluable reference point during negotiations. It serves as a baseline for evaluating proposals from other parties as well as the final outcomes. Having a firm grasp of the underlying economic and political rationale also provides material for making and defending arguments. In a negotiation situation, opponents try to talk the other out of their position, or attempt to catch them off-guard by asking questions they cannot answer. Having facts and figures that justifies one's position helps minimise these possibilities (Thompson 2012).

---

**Types of information needed for identifying national interests**

- National and regional policies on economic development, trade and industry;
- Detailed understanding of challenges and opportunities faced by domestic industries;
- Knowledge of the objectives your country is pursuing in other areas.

---

When establishing the aspiration point, it is important to be both realistic and optimistic. It is also crucial to go into significant depth. Studies of negotiations show that, all things being equal, negotiators with specific and ambitious aspiration points do better in negotiations than those with non-specific or low aspiration points (Malhotra and Bazerman 2007; Thompson 2012). Negotiators should stipulate as precisely as possible the desired outcomes, and the reasons why they are being sought. At this stage, it is important to think through prioritisation, in particular, which objectives might be sacrificed in order to obtain others, and areas in which concessions are not possible (Bhuglah 2004; Odell and Ortiz Mena 2004).

Three types of information are critical for identifying a country's negotiating objectives. First, the outcome of any trade negotiation should further national (and regional) policy objectives. Development plans and sector policies provide an invaluable guide for orienting negotiating objectives and determining priorities. As the agenda of trade negotiations expands to an ever-increasing range of 'behind the border' issues such as competition, investment and government procurement, detailed national and regional regulatory frameworks and legislation in these areas are indispensible for negotiating effectively.

Second, alongside national and regional policies, negotiators need very specific information about sub-sectors of the economy. Only with such detailed information is it possible to establish the specific changes to trade rules that can deliver commercially meaningful benefits. For each negotiation they enter, negotiators require the input of experts who know the current and likely future market conditions for the specific sub-sector (demand-side), the current and likely future competitiveness of local firms (supply-side) and the specific changes that negotiators should aim for. While this information might be gleaned from discussions with local firms and producers, in many instances negotiators will need to commission detailed assessments for each key sub-sector. These assessments can take several months to prepare.

Third, negotiators need to have information on how a specific negotiation relates to their country's wider foreign relations. They need to know what objectives their country's representatives are pursuing in other trade negotiations, to ensure that there is consistency. In the recent EPA negotiations with the EU, for instance, some African ambassadors stationed in Geneva were concerned that their countries' negotiating positions in EPAs were undermining their negotiating positions at the WTO. Consistency is often a particular problem with bilateral investment treaties, as these tend to not be negotiated as thoroughly and may contain obligations that are directly related to trade. Less obviously, negotiators need to ensure consistency with negotiations that are related to but not strictly focused on trade, including those with the World Bank, International Monetary Fund and other international organisations. Finally, negotiators need to know about wider diplomatic relationships and ongoing negotiations between their country and the others around the negotiating table. As a different ministry typically leads negotiations outside of trade, cross-government liaison is vital.

An acute lack of information is a challenge for many negotiators, particularly from the poorest developing countries. National development plans often have sections on trade that are scanty and provide little guidance. In addition detailed sector regulations and legislation are unavailable, and there is often a dearth of information on the possibilities for expansion of specific economic sectors. In such cases, it may be best to avoid negotiating until more information is available or national policies and legislation are in place. During the Doha Round, for instance, developing countries initially refused to negotiate on trade facilitation, and only after a thorough analysis they decided this was an area they would negotiate. Similarly, in the EPA negotiations, many African countries opted not to negotiate on areas such as competition and government procurement, because national and regional policies needed to be developed and implemented before they could make commitments towards the EU.

Overall, it is important not to underestimate the work involved in establishing your country's interests for each negotiation. The advice of expert negotiators chimes with the old saying 'act in haste, repent at leisure'. They caution that it is far better to take time to thoroughly understand your country's interests and determine negotiating objectives rather than negotiate without a full grasp of the issues on the table or clear negotiating objectives.

## Know the interests of your negotiating partners and relevant third parties

Gathering all relevant information on the interests of negotiating partners is essential. An intimate knowledge of all sets of interests at the table enables you to see where your interests conflict with those of your counterparties, and where your interests are complementary. This can assist with identifying possibilities for mutual gain. It also highlights areas where negotiations are likely to be relatively straightforward and areas where they may be fraught, and provides useful information on the type of negotiating strategy to select.

An understanding of the other parties' underlying interests can be of invaluable assistance for deciphering the bluff and rhetoric that is frequently used during negotiations. It can also help pre-empt such tactics. If you appear to the other parties to be thoroughly prepared and to have thoroughly researched your own interests and theirs, they are less likely to try and lie or manipulate information (Malhotra and Bazerman 2007).

A failure to thoroughly and objectively assess the interests of other parties is a common weakness in negotiations. During the TRIPS negotiations, for instance, the failure of developing countries to understand the business interests of pharmaceutical companies and other intellectual-property-intensive industries meant that they were taken by surprise at the expansive nature of the demands made by industrialised countries. A more thorough understanding of the business interests of the industrialised countries might have made them more prepared (Singh 2006).

*A failure to thoroughly and objectively assess the interests of other parties is a common weakness in negotiations.*

In assessing the interests of others, it is important to try and 'step into their shoes' and evaluate the information from their perspective. Each party comes to a negotiation with its own set of prejudices, assumptions and desires. What may appear to be a weak or insignificant factor when assessed from an external perspective may in fact be of great consequence to the other party. At this stage it is also helpful to ask, 'what choice am I asking them to make (from their perspective)?' This helps reveal the costs and benefits entailed for them in agreeing to your ideal outcomes, and may assist in packaging your proposal to make it most acceptable to the counterparty.

Assessing the negotiating interests of others can be challenging, not least because states often wish to hide their true interests for strategic reasons. As a result, their underlying interests may be significantly different from the positions that they state in the negotiating room. For this reason, serious effort needs to be invested into discovering the true interests of the other parties. Trade attachés and diplomatic staff posted in the partner country and relevant third countries can be an invaluable source of intelligence, as can businessmen and other strategically placed nationals living and working in that country. In the absence of diplomatic representatives, it may be possible to collaborate with other small countries that do have representatives and who have a common interest in obtaining such information.

Establishing a diplomatic presence is resource intensive and many small developing countries can only afford to post trade attachés in a few locations, so decisions on where to place these officials need to be taken carefully. Crucially, the importance of a location changes over time. In the past, the United States and EU were often the largest trading partners for developing countries, and along with Geneva, these were the common locations for countries to post their best trade attachés and negotiators. As the dynamics of trade and trade negotiations have shifted, countries have reassessed the strategic importance of these locations, and posted higher numbers of trade experts to the capitals of large emerging economies.

*What information should a country look for?* Before entering a negotiation, it is crucial to understand the motivations of the other parties, and the underlying reasons for them. Is your country the *demandeur* for the negotiation, and, if so, what might attract the other party to the negotiating table? Alternatively, if the other party is proposing the negotiations, what is their reason for wanting to negotiate? While direct economic gains are the most obvious rationale, the partner country might be proposing a trade negotiation in order to gain political support from your country in another forum (such as the United Nations), or it might want wish to negotiate in order to set a precedent for negotiations with others. This is important information, as it can provide an indication of how flexible the country is likely to be in the negotiating room. If it wants to solicit political support, then it is likely to be willing to grant significant concessions, whereas if it is hoping to set a precedent, then it is likely to propose a template text on a take-it-or-leave-it basis.

---

**Identifying the interests of other parties**

Which party is the *demandeur* of negotiations, and what is their motivation? How is this likely to shape their approach?

What do negotiating partners and third parties want from the negotiations? What do their politicians say in speeches? Is it possible to obtain their negotiating mandate?

What concessions have the other parties asked for in other recent negotiations? What concessions have they been reluctant to make?

Which interest groups in partner countries have a stake in the outcome? What appear to be their interests in the negotiations (from public statements, reports and so on)? How influential are they?

Which issues appear to be politically salient and hence likely to be 'red-lines' for the other parties?

---

Once motivations have been clarified, it is helpful to establish a thorough understanding of the underlying political economy of the partner country. This includes an understanding of the broad trade policy objectives of the government; knowledge of the various interest groups that have a stake in the negotiations and the degree to which they are actively lobbying and are likely to exert influence over government positions; appreciation of the institutional systems and decision-making processes in that country; and information on the concessions that the other party has made (and not made) in recent negotiations. This can help with the identification of potential allies, and enable better prediction of the negotiating partner's external strategy and response, helping to prevent agendas from 'sneaking up on you'.

Aside from this macro-level information, it is helpful to establish as much as possible about the other party's negotiating team and the individuals within it. What is the reputation and credibility of the team? How did they perform in the last set of negotiations, and how might this influence their approach? What is the hierarchy of decision-making? Who influences whom? What are the professional interests and ambitions of the key personalities? What might they be looking for from this negotiation on an individual level? Once the key decision makers have been identified, negotiators highlight the importance of cultivating a relationship with them from the outset, learning to read their body language and their ways of thinking.

The institutional context can differ markedly from country to country. In the United States, for instance, whether or not a system of fast-track authority is in place significantly influences the country's negotiating approach, as it determines the degree of leeway that the president has in trade negotiations. Crucially, the impeding expiry of fast track is likely to make the government eager to conclude the negotiations, and hence more willing to make concessions (Case Study 19). In Europe, understanding the division of competence in trade policy between the EU and member states in an issue area can help to gauge the likelihood of a concession being made (see the box 'EU competence in trade negotiations'). In terms of accessing information, the EU is remarkably open and porous, so sifting through the vast amount of available data and analysis is a major challenge for developing countries seeking to identify the EU's interests (Goodison 2010).

---

**EU competence in trade negotiations**

*EU has exclusive competence in*:

- Trade in goods (tariffs, rules of origin, sanitary and phytosanitary measures and technical barriers to trade);

- Trade in services (although concessions in audiovisual, health, education and social services need the unanimous backing of member states);
- Trade-related intellectual property rights;
- Foreign direct investment (liberalisation and investment protection);
- Government procurement;
- Competition policy;
- Trade facilitation.

*Member states have exclusive competence in*:

- Portfolio investment;
- Aid for trade and development finance;
- Migration.

*Source*: Woolcock (2010).

While there is a vast academic and policy literature documenting the factors that influence EU and US approaches to trade negotiations, far less information is available to assist with preparations for negotiating with large developing countries. Moreover, while conventional wisdom suggests that they are more likely to be flexible towards small developing countries than industrialised countries, this expectation is increasingly outdated. Discussions with several developing country negotiators suggest that, in the area of bilateral investment treaties, China is a more stringent and demanding negotiator than the United States.[3] This underscores the need to prepare just as thoroughly when entering negotiations with large developing countries.

The extensive preparation that Costa Rica undertook for negotiations on financial services in the context of FTA negotiations between Central America and the United States (Dominican Republic Central America Free Trade Agreement) provides a valuable example of the steps to take in establishing one's own interests, as well as those of other parties (Case Study 2).

**Case Study 2: Costa Rica's extensive preparations for financial services negotiations with the United States**

In 2003, Costa Rica and other countries in Central America embarked on free trade agreement negotiations with the United

States (DR-CAFTA). This included the liberalisation of financial services, an issue that was politically contentious in Costa Rica. As Costa Rica's lead negotiator for financial services explains 'substantive preparation was pivotal...the key for a successful negotiation was to avoid any surprise during the negotiation process'.

In preparing for negotiations, Costa Rica's negotiators defined precise negotiating objectives in each issue area that responded to the economic and political realities, were realistic, and would not generate misleading expectations among any sector of the Costa Rican constituency. They gathered extensive information in order to anticipate how the negotiations in each issue area would evolve and to envisage the most likely scenarios that they would face in the later stages of the process. This included anticipating the positions and texts the United States would submit to the negotiation table; the advantages and disadvantages of every proposal for Costa Rica; identifying which issues were going to be the most controversial; and devising a strategy to lead the conclusion of the negotiations to the most politically digestible outcome.

Information was gathered from many sources. Negotiators:

- examined the legal frameworks for financial services in Costa Rica and the United States, including recent jurisprudential developments and bills under consideration in both Congresses;
- identified relevant pressure groups both in Costa Rica and in the United States; analysed the legal texts of each financial services chapter negotiated by the United States in each of its free trade agreements, particularly the most recent;
- scrutinised the United States' commitments under General Agreement on Trade in Services (GATS);
- searched for and analysed comments that US financial businesses had made about the Costa Rican financial sector;
- reviewed the reports of major international organizations on the Costa Rican financial services framework and various studies on the strengths and weaknesses of the insurance monopoly in Costa Rica.

*Source*: Echandi (2006: 42).

## Establish your best possible alternative but do not reveal it

A crucial lesson for developing countries is that in a negotiation, power is not determined by aggregate resource levels (such as the size of the market) but rather the relative power of parties in a given issue area, their desire to reach an agreement and their ability and will to use these resources effectively. In any negotiation, a negotiator's 'best alternative to a negotiated agreement' or BATNA is their most important source of power (Fisher and Ury 1991; Thompson 2012). Simply put, the more powerful country is usually the one that has the most attractive alternative options and can walk away most easily. As Hirschman noted as far back as 1945, however asymmetrical the negotiation might be in terms of aggregate resource levels, if a relatively small developing country can obtain equivalent benefits from a third party outside of the negotiation, or take other steps to minimise the harm incurred from walking away, then the large state has little hold over it (Hirschman 1945).

*Simply put, the more powerful country is usually the one that has the most attractive alternative options and can walk away most easily.*

Before entering a negotiation, it is imperative that a negotiator knows their BATNA, and has evaluated it as objectively as possible. Once the BATNA is clear, a 'walk-away' point or set of 'red-lines' can be determined, beyond which it is better for the country to exit the negotiations rather than make any further concessions. It is also crucial that a negotiator does not reveal their BATNA or 'walk-away' point to the other side; this is an unwise move even in the friendliest of situations. When the other side knows the point at which you will walk away, they have no incentive to offer anything more than this (Thompson 2012: 70).

While it is important that negotiators do not reveal their BATNA to the other party, it is equally important that the other party sees them as ultimately being able and willing to walk away. When the counterpart perceives a credible increase in the willingness of the other party to walk away, the concessions that they are willing to make often improve (Lax and Sebenius 2006: 87). For this reason, it may be helpful to drop hints that alternatives are available, without revealing details. For instance, a negotiator may hint that talks with third parties are underway and advancing rapidly.

For the weaker side in a negotiation, determining this 'walk-away' point is extremely important as adhering to it protects a state from entering an unfavourable agreement (Fisher and Ury 1991). During its negotiations with the EU, for instance, Bolivia decided to walk away when it became clear that the EU was insistent on the inclusion of TRIPS-plus provisions, a red-line for Bolivia (Gray Molina 2010). Similarly, the Pacific walked away from negotiating services with the EU in the context of EPAs, on the grounds that agreeing to the EU's terms would set a negative precedent for negotiations with Australia and New Zealand (Case Study 3). Yet, all too often in complex situations, even experienced bargainers spend most of their time focusing on what they want to achieve and the intricacies of the negotiation and little time planning what they would do in the event of no deal (Odell 2010: 553).

---

### Identifying alternatives

Is the current position sustainable? Is doing nothing an option; if so, for how long?

Is there an alternative market to promote?

Is there a multilateral/bilateral alternative?

Is there a choice between negotiating as a country or as part of a region?

Are other trade instruments available for obtaining your objectives (trade preferences, for instance)?

Could these objectives be met through the use of domestic policies?

---

To identify their BATNA and 'walk-away' point, negotiators should brainstorm the full range of alternative options available to their country in the event that negotiations end in impasse and evaluate the merits of each. In a complex negotiation, covering many issue areas, it may be helpful to identify several 'packages', equivalent in value, which represent the walk-away point. Often negotiators set arbitrary limits on individual issues (for instance, setting a maximum percentage of trade that will be liberalised). However, this reduces the negotiator's flexibility. To create 'packages' it is helpful to ask, in each issue area, is this limit a non-negotiable 'red-line', or is it something on which we would be prepared to make a concession if the other party compensated in other areas? If the latter, how large would we need these concessions to be?

It may seem obvious that a negotiator should be willing to accept any set of terms superior to their best alternative and reject outcomes that are worse than it, yet negotiators often fail on both counts. They assume that their alternatives are better than they really are, or they are manipulated by negative information into thinking that their best alternative is worse than it really is. To guard against these problems, negotiators need to establish their best alternative prior to a negotiation, to keep their options open during negotiation by cultivating alternatives and continually assess their BATNA on the basis of objective facts and evidence. In particular, they should not be swayed by information from the other side. Indeed, the party that stands to gain most from changing our mind in a negotiation should be the least persuasive (Thompson 2012: 35–36).

During a negotiation, it can be hard for a negotiator to determine whether their BATNA is better than any other offer that the other party will make. However, there are signs to look for which will suggest when 'no deal' is likely to be the best outcome (see the box 'Signs that "no deal" is the best outcome').

*What should a negotiator do if their BATNA is weak?* There is nothing that creates more anxiety for negotiators than the feeling of desperation that comes from having no good alternatives. However, having a weak BATNA is not terribly problematic if the other side does not know that your BATNA is weak. While this may sound obvious, a common mistake of negotiators is to unwittingly reveal the weakness of their BATNA, for instance, by appearing extremely eager to meet, and for negotiations to progress (Malhotra and Bazerman 2007: 238–239).

Beyond this, it is crucial to do everything possible to improve your BATNA and to ensure that it is ready to be implemented if needed. Indeed, this is probably the most significant step that can be taken to increase negotiating power, particularly when negotiating from a position of relative weakness (Fisher and Ury 1991; Salacuse 2000; HBSP 2005; Thompson 2012).

---

**Signs that 'no deal' is the best outcome**

You have told them about your other offers and they are unable to match or beat them;

Instead of trying to match your needs, they are trying to convince you that your interests are not what they really are;

They seem more interested in stretching out the negotiation than in exchanging information, or structuring an agreement;

Despite your best efforts, they will not answer any of your questions; nor will they ask about your needs or interests.

*Source*: Malhotra and Bazerman (2007: 294–295).

*What kind of alternatives might a trade negotiator look for and cultivate?* The most basic alternative to entering into a new agreement is to simply go without an agreement in favour of the status quo. However, this is not always possible. In some situations, large states have the power to remove the status quo option. For instance, during the EPA negotiations the EU withdrew Cotonou trade preferences, which meant that the status quo option was no longer available to some African, Caribbean and Pacific (ACP) states. Alternatively, the status quo option can be eliminated if large states enter into FTAs with competitors, leaving the smaller country 'out in the cold' (Gruber 2001). The FTA between the United States and Singapore was one of the main reasons that Thailand sought an FTA with the United States. Thailand hoped that an FTA would help to neutralise the competitive advantages that Singapore had gained (Pupphavesa et al. 2011).

To strengthen their hand, negotiators may be able to find alternative trade partners who are willing to offer an agreement that is better than the status quo option. This can be useful even if the alternate agreement is less than they hope to obtain through the ongoing negotiation. This tactic is often used by large states. During the negotiations over the formation of General Agreement on Tariffs and Trade in the 1940s, for instance, while the United States was the stronger economic power, the United Kingdom had significant leverage over the terms of the new regime because it had better alternative options, in the form of extensive trade relations with its commonwealth and empire. The presence of a strong alternative option led the United States to make significant concessions to keep the United Kingdom on board. Later, in the 1980s, the United States used the recent conclusion of a bilateral trade agreement with Canada as a threat to other trading partners that it might abandon the multilateral trading system in favour of bilateral agreements, and this helped jump-start the Uruguay Round (Odell and Eichengreen 1998).

**Case Study 3: Knowing when to say 'no': services negotiations between Pacific Island States and the EU**

In 2002, the Pacific ACP states entered Economic Partnership Agreement negotiations with the EU. A clear identification of their alternatives and 'walk-away' point in the area of services enabled the Pacific states to decide when it was appropriate to stop negotiating and exit from the negotiations. Thus they avoided setting a negative precedent for future negotiations with other trading partners.

In the area of services, Pacific states adopted a position that was largely defensive, proposing a draft text that included a range of 'development safeguards' to ensure that any agreement with the EU would not unduly restrict their ability to regulate their domestic services. The one notable exception was the temporary migration of natural persons (Mode 4), where the Pacific states requested increased access to the EU labour market. Significant concessions in this area would have provided valuable access to the European market, and, importantly, would have been of great strategic importance in setting a favourable precedent for subsequent negotiations with Australia and New Zealand.

The Pacific states identified concessions in Mode 4 as a redline for the negotiations. After several rounds of negotiations, it became clear that while the EU sought significant services liberalisation commitments for Pacific ACP states, it was unwilling to provide concessions in Mode 4 that Pacific states considered meaningful. In response, the Pacific states opted to walk out of negotiations on services, making it clear that negotiations could only continue if the EU was willing to alter its position. In a letter to the European Trade Commissioner, Hans Joachim Keil, the Ministerial Spokesperson for the Pacific states said, '[W]hat has been offered by the EC and EU Member States in regard to trade in services... does not satisfy the fundamental concerns of the [Pacific ACP states] at this time. Given that situation, our region proposes that negotiations on trade in services be suspended for the time being and a rendezvous clause be included in the EPA that would commit both sides to revisit services... in the future.'

*Source*: Correspondence from Hon Joe Keil, Lead Spokesperson for PACP Trade Ministers, to Peter Mandelson, EC Commissioner for Trade, 11 June 2008; Julian et al. (2007).

## Identify other sources of potential leverage

While a strong BATNA is the most potent source of power in a negotiation, other sources of leverage are often available to developing countries. Before embarking on a negotiation, it is helpful to audit potential sources of leverage. Subsequent chapters of the guide consider how they can be used to best effect.

---

**Potential sources of leverage**

- Control over resources such as raw materials, minerals, land and water that are in high demand;
- Land that is strategic in military or geopolitical terms;
- UN votes;
- Diplomatic recognition;
- Forming coalitions or alliances with others;
- Access to information and ideas;
- Ability to make moral arguments;
- Personal qualities of negotiators;
- Large states may have weak BATNAs;
- Large states underestimating resolve and capacity of smaller developing countries.

---

Influence can sometimes be derived from control over resources that the other party considers to be of strategic importance, and it is worth considering whether these can be added to the negotiation, or otherwise linked to its outcome. During the Lomé negotiations in the early 1970s, for instance, ACP countries extracted significant concessions from Europe because they were exporters of raw materials that Europe needed.

In recent years, industrialised countries have become acutely concerned about securing their access to rare earth metals. These metals are essential to various production processes in industrialised economies, including the manufacture of high-tech weaponry, making access to them a matter of national security. Although rare earth metals are of great strategic value to the United States and EU, China controls more than 90 per cent of these metals, and is keen to preserve them for its own manufacturing. Deposits have recently been found in small African states including Mozambique, Zambia and Burundi and these deposits provide them with a potential bargaining chip for trade negotiations with the EU and the United States, on whom they are otherwise highly dependent for aid and trade. As countries become increasingly concerned about securing access to food, land and water resources are also becoming valuable bargaining chips.

In some negotiations, developing countries may be able to leverage political or military resources. They may be able to use their vote in the UN, particularly if they are negotiating as a group and can coordinate voting positions. Alternatively, they may be able to take advantage of a diplomatic rivalry between their negotiating partner and third parties. During the 1990s, for instance, many African states used the intense rivalry between China and Taiwan to strategic effect, using decisions over diplomatic recognition of Taiwan in order to secure concessions from both sides.

Aside from these resource-based sources of leverage, a variety of tactical moves that provide leverage. Forming coalitions or entering into strategic alliances with other countries or non-state actors can often increase the influence of a weaker party in a negotiation. Alternatively, information and ideas can also be important sources of power: if negotiators from small developing country are able to make their case on the basis of compelling and irrefutable facts, evidence or legal expertise, they may be able to reveal inconsistencies in the arguments of the other party or shift the way in which the other party perceives its interests and approaches the negotiation. In some instances, negotiators can derive a high level of leverage by shaping public opinion in their favour. Finally, personal qualities may be a source of power: a negotiator who has high level of technical expertise and political nous can often exert greater influence over outcomes than negotiators who lack these qualities. The tactical moves that make uses of these potential sources of power are examined in detail in subsequent chapters.

Paradoxically, in some cases smallness or having low levels of income can be turned to a country's advantage in the negotiating room. Rendered complacent by the disparity in the size of human and material resources, the stronger party might not fully examine the other side's power potential with regard to the specific issues under negotiation. Larger parties sometimes fail to grasp the degree of commitment and priority that the smaller side has placed on achieving a particular end. Moreover, size and complexity may also mean that the large state may allocate fewer resources to devote to a negotiation than first envisaged, and it may be easily distracted by other events. Provided that it has the requisite expertise, a small state may be able to devote more focused attention and have a clearer strategy for negotiations, giving it a significant advantage (Salacuse 2000). Indeed, this is arguably what gave Costa Rica the edge in a WTO dispute with the United States (Case Study 4).

---

**Case Study 4: The large player underestimates the resolve of the small: Costa Rica wins trade dispute with the United States**

In the mid-1990s, the United States claimed that its domestic underwear industry was being seriously damaged by imported and human-made fibre underwear from Costa Rica and six other countries. After initial consultations, three countries agreed to quantitative restrictions on their exports of underwear, and further discussions led to a settlement with Honduras, Thailand and Turkey. However, the United States and Costa Rica were unable to reach a negotiated agreement. After intense discussions among internal stakeholders, Costa Rica decided to initiate dispute settlement proceedings at the WTO.

Costa Rica prevailed in both the dispute settlement process and the subsequent legal appeal, and the United States accepted and conformed to the rulings. One of the factors contributing to Costa Rica's success was that the United States appeared to underestimate Costa Rica's resolve and its capacity to prosecute the case, expecting it to back down as others had done. When the case went before the dispute settlement panel, many discrepancies emerged in the information provided by the United States, which undermined the credibility of its claim. The Costa Rican team handling the case believed that if the United States had seriously thought that a dispute settlement panel would eventually scrutinise the data, they would have taken much more care in preparing their case.

*Source*: Breckenridge (2005).

---

## Establish the other party's alternatives and sources of leverage

Knowing the alternatives available to other parties, and hence their 'walk-away' point, is extremely valuable information in a negotiation.

Mapping the point at which both parties will walk away enables negotiators to identify whether there is sufficient overlap in the interests of the parties for an agreement to be made.

Comparing the walk-away points of the parties at the table reveals what is referred to in the negotiating literature as the 'zone of possible agreement' (ZOPA). In some cases, where there is no overlap in interests, such a zone may not exist. A simple example illustrates this point. If, in a bilateral negotiation on services, country A wants to liberalise a maximum of two services sub-sectors and will walk out rather than commit more, while country B will only sign up to an agreement that that includes the liberalisation of five or more services sub-sectors, then negotiations will be challenging. The parties can try and create a 'zone of agreement' by working hard to try and change each other's preferences and hence their red-lines. But if this is not possible, then they may both be better off walking away and investing energies elsewhere.

In other situations, there may indeed be a clear 'zone of possible agreement'. If, for instance, country C wants to liberalise a maximum of five sub-sectors, while country D is prepared to sign an agreement that includes liberalisation of two or more sub-sectors, then there is a clear zone of possible agreement, which lies between these two points. The challenge for negotiators is to determine where, within this range, the final outcome will fall.

Even more importantly, knowledge of the other party's alternatives and walk-away point is key to claiming value. Following the example above, if negotiators from country C know that the minimum country D will accept is the liberalisation of two sub-sectors, then even if the other party is much larger, they can make this offer and stick to it, confident that country D will eventually concede.

Accurately, diagnosing relative power positions in a negotiation by comparing the alternatives and walk-away points is vital information for developing a negotiating strategy. For instance, if a large state is desperately seeking access to a particular rare earth metal and the small country concerned is the sole supplier, the latter is in a powerful position. If, on the other hand, the small country is one of several sources of the metal, then however important that metal is to the large state, it is in a less powerful position. Such information should inform the negotiating strategy: the most effective negotiators are those who adjust their behaviour in accordance with the relative power position of the other side (Zartman and Rubin 2000: 284).

*The most effective negotiators are those who adjust their behaviour in accordance with the relative power position of the other side.*

As the other party has every reason to conceal their walk-away point and alternatives, these can be hard to assess. However, as one expert advises 'do not leave any stone unturned when attempting to assess the counterparty's BATNA' (Thompson 2012: 175).

---

**Potential sources of leverage for large countries**

- Unilateral trade preferences;
- Aid;
- Concessional loans;
- Foreign direct investment;
- Control of key information.

---

In some cases, countries have used third parties to gather sensitive information. During the NAFTA negotiations, for instance, Mexico hired US lobbyists, which enabled it to have first-hand information on US interests and walk-away point. It also meant that the United States could not credibly bluff in order to extract concessions (Ortiz Mena 2006). When negotiating with countries where lobbying is less common, it may be possible to draw on the expertise of local law firms that have an intimate knowledge of the decision-making processes and that are familiar with the key actors. However, using third parties can be an expensive option, and due diligence is needed to ensure that the third party can be fully trusted and their information is credible.

In asymmetric trade negotiations, the ability of a large state to withdraw aid, concessional loans and trade preferences from the small state can provide them with significant additional leverage. As one negotiator explains, 'large states have many sources of power and they do not hesitate to use them'.[4] A thorough and realistic assessment of these sources of power, anticipation of how and when the large state is likely to use them and evaluation of the costs that they would impose is a really important step in developing an effective negotiating strategy.

Interviews suggest that negotiators from small developing countries often perceive themselves to be negotiating under high levels of threat, particularly fearing the withdrawal of aid and trade preferences. Crucially, threats did not always need to be made explicitly to be effective, as many negotiators perceive a high risk of retaliation in these areas if they do not comply with the demands of the large state (Jones et al. 2010: 64). A motivating factor in Thailand's decision to embark on FTA negotiations with the United States was that the latter had threatened to withdraw unilateral trade preferences because Thailand had failed to implement intellectual property rights to a level that the United States considered satisfactory (Pupphavesa et al. 2011: 172).

When preparing to negotiate, it is important that small developing countries thoroughly assess the likelihood of any threats being made, their likely credibility and the precise impact that they would have on the domestic economy. During negotiations, parties have every incentive to manipulate perceptions of their relative power position, exaggerating both their ability to carry out a threat and its likely impact (Odell and Ortiz Mena 2004). In assessing the credibility of potential threats, it is helpful to understand the political and legislative processes entailed in carrying out a threat. For instance, a trade negotiator may imply that aid will be cut if a particular trade concession is not made, yet this threat is only credible if there is backing from the wider government. Investigations may reveal that a donor government may not be willing to sacrifice a flagship aid project for the sake of a relatively minor trade concession.

Knowledge of alternatives and red-lines is also crucial when negotiating with foreign investors. A common negotiating tactic used by foreign investors is to threaten to relocate their operations unless the government changes regulations that the investor considers unfavourable or provides incentives such as tax concessions or infrastructure. In anticipation of such arguments, prior knowledge of the costs to the firm of relocating and the concessions and regulations available in other locations can be invaluable. Similarly, if a foreign investor threatens international arbitration if a government enacts a particular policy, it is important that host governments evaluate the credibility of the threat, determining the cost of arbitration for the company and the likelihood of the company winning a case. Detailed assessment enabled Costa Rica to successfully call the bluff of one multinational that threatened arbitration (Case Study 5).

---

**Case Study 5: Knowing the other party's walk-away point: Costa Rica and a US Oil Company**

In the late 1990s, Harken Costa Rica Holdings, a subsidiary of a US oil company, obtained a concession agreement to drill for oil off Costa Rica's Caribbean coast, including the environmentally sensitive Talamanca region. Drilling was contingent on the outcome of an environmental impact assessment.

The impact assessment carried out by Harken was heavily criticised; the Costa Rican environmental agency identified numerous legal and technical shortcomings and decided not to give its approval. In response, Harken filed a request for international arbitration, claiming it had lost US$9–$12 million in exploration activity and costs related to administrative and legal procedures. It sought US$57 billion in damages and lost future profits.

Rather than immediately agree to a costly international arbitration process, Costa Rica carefully studied the wider legal context and decided that the company was in a weak position. This enabled the president to confidently call the bluff of the company, flatly refusing international arbitration, and pointing out that Harken's contract required it to exhaust local remedies before resorting to international processes. Furthermore, he argued that the company had not met its environmental requirements, which was a clear basis for terminating the contract. Only 17 days after the initial request for international arbitration, Harken dropped the case as a 'good faith' act and sought negotiations. These were unsuccessful, and in a resolution signed by the president, the government of Costa Rica formally cancelled Harken's concession contract.

*Source*: Tienhaara (2008).

## Secure high-level political buy-in

Once a thorough diagnosis of an upcoming negotiation has been made, including the identification of interests, specific negotiating objectives, and sources of potential leverage, it is vital that buy-in is obtained from the most senior levels. This serves three broad purposes. First, and perhaps most obviously, having a mandate that is endorsed by the highest level of government provides negotiators with very clear direction. Second, it strengthens the level of accountability between the negotiator and the wider government, as it provides a set of objectives against which negotiators' performance can be evaluated. Third, and crucially for the smaller country in a negotiation, it can increase political leverage.

Buy-in is often obtained by senior government officials, relevant ministers, and possibly the cabinet approving a negotiating mandate before negotiations commence. A mandate typically sets out the negotiating objectives, the red-lines or areas where the country will not make concessions, and the degree of authority that is delegated to negotiators. It is often accompanied by an explanatory memorandum, which sets out the rationale for the negotiating objectives. Mandates may be vague and only offer broad guidance, leaving the negotiator with a relatively high level of discretion, or they may be very detailed, setting out very specific targets and leaving the negotiator with very little flexibility. As they contain sensitive information that would greatly undermine negotiating leverage if accessed by opponents, mandates are usually closely guarded.

Depending on the importance of the negotiation, members of the negotiating team may be required to report back to senior officials and the executive frequently for additional direction, or they may be given a relatively high degree of autonomy and discretion. In general, regular reporting is a key part of ensuring effective oversight and accountability of negotiators. This process informs the senior levels of government of the progress being made and provides negotiators with the opportunity to request further guidance and/or high-level political intervention.

As discussed in subsequent chapters, large states use a variety of tactics, including putting pressure on the executive branch of government. Having a mandate approved by the whole cabinet helps lock in the sector minister and head of state, making it less likely that the country will settle for a poor deal. Having an approved mandate can embolden negotiators, as it enables them to identify issue-areas where they can adopt a strong negotiating position, secure in the knowledge that they have the support of the executive. This is particularly important given evidence that negotiators are sometimes reluctant to take a strong stand in negotiations for fear that they might be used as a scapegoat by their superiors in the event that a powerful opponent issues threats (Jones et al. 2010: 62).

## Develop sound negotiating proposals

Once negotiators have a clear idea of what is being asked of them, they can start translating their negotiating objectives into technical proposals and draft texts. Drafting legal texts that are economically and legally sound is complex and time consuming, and so, many small developing countries do not invest in developing their own proposals, reacting instead to the texts proposed by their negotiating partners. As a result, they negotiate defensively from the outset, which makes it hard to secure their offensive interests.

In drafting texts, it is useful to consider existing legal precedents as this can help bolster your position, a move that is particularly applicable when negotiating at the bilateral level. Large countries typically negotiate from template or model texts, and the smaller party can scrutinise previous agreements that the negotiating partner has entered into, to identify the most advantageous provisions that it has agreed to elsewhere, and develop their proposals around these. Alternately, smaller parties can learn from the negative experiences of others and avoid certain provisions or ensure they are drafted differently.

International organisations have undertaken significant research and analysis into treaties, and made proposals for alternative drafting language, including in the area of investment (see the box 'Resources for drafting legal texts on investment'). For instance, a criticism of some model treaties used by industrialised countries is that they adopt a very broad definition of investment, which means the provisions of the treaty can be applied to anything from sovereign debt to portfolio investment. Through the use of 'narrowing techniques' during the drafting of texts, developing country negotiators can limit the reach of investment treaties. They might use a closed-list definition (where the treaty only covers what is listed) instead of an open one (everything is covered, except what is listed); explicitly exclude portfolio shares, sovereign debt, and certain other types of assets; and take a very selective approach to intellectual property rights as assets (UNCTAD 2011). Having this type of drafting guidance at hand before and during negotiations can be invaluable.

---

**Resources for drafting legal texts on investment**

- IISD (International Institute for Sustainable Development) Model International Agreement on Investment for Sustainable Development (2005), available at www.iisd.org;

- UNCTAD Investment Policy Framework for Sustainable Development (2012), available at www.unctad.org;

- UNCTAD 'Pink Series' – providing guidance on key provisions in international investment agreements, such as Most Favored Nation, Fair and Equitable Treatment and Expropriation, available at www.unctad.org;

- Commonwealth Secretariat Investment Guide for Negotiators (2012), available at www.thecommonwealth.org.

# Summary

Thorough preparation takes substantial effort and resources, but this initial investment can have a high pay-off. Key preparatory steps include establishing the best possible negotiating team as early as possible in the negotiating process; identifying national interests and setting realistic yet ambitious negotiating objectives; investigating the underlying interests of the other parties at the table, and establishing a nuanced understanding of the political economy behind their negotiating positions; exploring the sources of leverage available to each party, including the strength of each party's BATNA and the point at which each side will walk away; taking steps to improve your own BATNA; and, finally, codifying this diagnosis into a negotiating mandate, securing political buy-in and preparing draft texts.

Crucially, if the negotiating team has adequately prepared, they will have a solid understanding of the relative power position of the parties. This will make them less likely to be manipulated by the other side and more likely to be able to claim substantial value during the course of the negotiations.

In the next chapter, we turn to examine the tactical moves that can be made during a negotiation, starting with those made 'away from the table'.

---

**Checklist: Preparation and Diagnosis**

**What are our interests?** What are our top negotiating objectives and priorities, political as well as economic? What issues are negotiable/non-negotiable?

**What are the interests of the other parties?** What are they likely to ask for? What issues will they be seeking to keep off the table and why?

**Which interest groups have a stake in the outcomes?** Which groups are potential allies? Which groups have the potential to disrupt negotiations or undermine our position?

**What is our best alternative to a negotiated agreement?** What would we do if the talks end in impasse, and how attractive or awful is that course of action? How can alternative options be strengthened?

**What do the other parties' perceive as their best alternatives?** Given this, what is the worst deal they would probably accept?

**From the initial diagnosis, is it possible to envisage a possible range of agreements?** Are our goals totally in conflict with those of the other party, largely complementary or some mixture?

**What are the sources of leverage available to us?** How might we use them?

**What are the sources of leverage available to the other parties?** How are they likely to use them?

**Have we secured high-level political buy-in?** Have we drafted legal texts that reflect our offensive and defensive interests?

# 3
# Moves Away from the Negotiating Table

Many of the most important tactical moves taken in a negotiation occur 'away from the table'. Such moves are vital for setting up the most promising situation *at* the negotiating table. Indeed, if negotiators do not seek to influence the negotiating set-up, they are likely to be placed at an inherent disadvantage. In the words of two experts, '[N]o matter how many right moves you make at the table – however skilfully you read body language, build trust, frame arguments, make offers and counter offers – doing so at the wrong table can undercut your results' (Lax and Sebenius 2004).

Key decisions about the set-up are taken *before* the parties sit down at the table. Through emails, telephone calls and informal one-on-one meetings, critical aspects of the negotiation are decided. These decisions include who will be at the negotiating table, where the negotiations will be held, the rules and decision-making procedures that will be followed, and the issues on the agenda and sequence in which they will be addressed.

Influencing these initial decisions can have an impact on the final outcome. In addition, initial interactions provide an excellent opportunity to learn as much as possible about the expectations and interests of negotiating partners (Bhuglah 2004).

Tactical moves away from the table are also useful once formal negotiations have started. This is particularly true for international trade negotiations which can last for many years. Moves include forming coalitions and alliances, shaping public opinion, and actively managing domestic politics.

## Select the most favourable forum

The decision over the forum in which a negotiation takes place can strongly affect gains and losses, as it influences who will participate, the rules of the game and how any resulting agreement will be enforced.

Industrialised countries actively use 'forum-shifting' to advance their negotiating objectives. A common strategy has been to switch between negotiations at the multilateral and bilateral level. In 2003, after the failure of the fifth WTO ministerial meeting in Cancun, for instance, the United States openly announced it would pursue its interests at the bilateral level, negotiating free trade agreements with 'can-do' countries, a move that would enable it to use asymmetrical bargaining power to greater effect. Similarly, the push to shift the negotiations on intellectual property from the United Nations to the WTO worked to the interests of industrialised countries as it provided a far stronger mechanism for enforcement (Devereaux et al. 2006b). More recently, as the negotiating strength of developing countries in the area of intellectual property has increased, industrialised countries are shifting decision-making to new fora where they can advance their interests more easily (Case Study 6).

Vigilance on the part of developing countries is crucial for defending against such 'forum-shifting' tactics. In particular, countries need to ensure there is excellent coordination and communication among those representing their country in different negotiations. A valuable lesson from Case Study 6 is that steps need to be taken to improve the political oversight of officials participating in negotiations in areas such as customs and standards setting, which have traditionally been seen as purely technical, and to ensure that these officials have greater awareness of the broader trade priorities and concerns of their government.

It is particularly difficult for small developing countries to react effectively to forum-shifting, as they are not always represented in all the relevant fora. Active networks among developing countries can be invaluable for mitigating this constraint. Barbados, for instance, works within an informal network of small country delegations in Geneva, including other Caribbean countries, Singapore and Mauritius, and they 'watch each other's back'. As one senior official explained, 'They call us if we are not present in the room and they think our interests may be compromised'. This informal network functions across negotiating fora and extends into non-trade areas (Jones et al. 2010: 50).

---

**Case Study 6: Forum-shifting undermines developing country opposition: the enforcement of intellectual property rights**

Intellectual property has become one of the most hotly contested areas of international trade negotiations, with industrialised countries advocating stricter rules and levels of enforcement, many of which are strongly opposed by developing countries. In the past, the World Trade Organization and World Intellectual Property Organization were the primary focal points for discussing intellectual property rights, but the proposals of industrialised countries met with strong opposition from developing countries. As a result, industrialised countries are increasingly turning their attention to other organisations, and with some success.

The World Customs Organization (WCO) is one such organisation. Although the WCO is mandated to support its member states to implement the WTO TRIPS Agreement, in practice it has promoted stricter enforcement, focusing on the exchange of 'best practices' (based on high standards adopted by only a few states) and on the provision of technical assistance that encourages countries to go beyond TRIPS. In 2007, under the auspices of the WCO, industrialised countries proposed the codification of these 'best practices' through the creation of a framework on standards, which would ensure higher levels of enforcement across all 178 member states of the WCO. Although this went beyond TRIPS provisions, developing countries did not raise much opposition. Only at the last minute, after several discussions of the draft framework, one developing country delegation realised its significance and successfully mobilised a small coalition to block its approval.

A similar trend is discernable at the Universal Postal Union (UPU), a technical organisation responsible for global cooperation among postal services. In 2008, a proposal to prohibit counterfeit and pirated articles being sent by post was voted on and passed without significant debate or opposition from developing countries. As a result, there is now a prohibition on sending counterfeit and pirated articles by post (in stark contrast, there is no mention, restriction or prohibition in relation to weapons).

Why, when they have vehemently opposed similar proposals at the WTO, have developing countries shown far less opposition at the WCO and UPU? The shift of forum away from the World Trade Organization and World Intellectual Property Organization puts developing countries at a distinct disadvantage. The World Customs Organization and the Universal Postal Union are characterised by higher levels of informal governance and issues are compartmentalised and dealt with on purely technical grounds. As the delegates of developing countries are typically drawn from customs and postal services, they are not versed in the wider technical and political debates over intellectual property and are unaware of their far-reaching implications. In addition, as a result of the informal governance structures developing countries are often poorly represented. For instance, small steering groups, which do not proportionally represent the member states, take many of the key decisions.

*Source*: Guimarães de Lima e Silva (2012).

In some instances, developing country negotiators may be able to actively influence the choice of forum in their favour, opting to negotiate in a forum where the rules and procedures are known to work to their benefit (or at least where there is less potential for bias against them). A series of studies suggest that it is often preferable for small developing countries to pursue negotiations in a multilateral setting rather than a bilateral one, as power asymmetries are tempered by systematic rules and procedures, and small developing countries have the opportunity to form coalitions. Indeed, one of the reasons African countries have cited for not negotiating on issues such as government procurement in free trade agreements is that they are waiting for these issues to be negotiated at the WTO, a forum in which they arguably stand a better chance of securing rules that reflect their interests.

> *It is often preferable for small developing countries to pursue negotiations in a multilateral setting . . . , as power asymmetries are tempered by systematic rules and procedures, and small developing countries have the opportunity to form coalitions.*

Simply getting a larger trading partner to engage in substantive negotiations over an issue they are concerned about can pose a challenge for developing countries. Here again the multilateral setting can have advantages. In a member-based organisation such as the WTO, the vast majority of trading partners are already at the table, and it is arguably easier for small countries to put an issue on the agenda, not least because they can form coalitions. The dispute settlement mechanism of the WTO can be a particularly effective way of compelling larger states into negotiations and, if this fails, into adjudication. This is illustrated in the experiences of Peru and Vietnam, which used different routes to try and obtain changes in the labelling policies of their key trading partners, with very different outcomes (Case Study 7).

### Case Study 7: The advantages of multilateralism: Peru and Vietnam seeking changes in trade policies

Peru and Vietnam both faced policies in their key export markets that discriminated against their exports. Peru faced labelling problems that impeded its access to the European Union (EU) market for scallops and sardines, while Vietnam faced labelling problems and anti-dumping actions that reduced catfish exports to the United States. While Peru was able to pursue changes to EU policy through the WTO, as a non-WTO member Vietnam had to rely on bilateral approaches to try and obtain a change in US policy.

*Peru*

Following the enforcement of EU labelling rules on sardine imports in the late 1990s, Peru tried for two years to reach a negotiated settlement through bilateral contacts at all political levels, but the EU refused to compromise on its position. Unable to reach a negotiated settlement, Peru filed a complaint at the WTO, forcing the EU to the negotiating table. When consultations failed, the case went to a WTO Panel, which ruled in favour of Peru. The EU appealed against the decision, but lost. After the legal case, Peru and the EU parties still had to negotiate an acceptable agreement; however, the WTO legal ruling provided Peru with leverage and was essential in getting a favourable outcome. In the words of one Peruvian official 'winning the panel ruling opens space for negotiation and strengthens our position'.

*Vietnam*

The contrast with Vietnam's experience of trying to obtain a change in US policies is striking. The two countries had entered a bilateral trade agreement in 2000, which led to a surge in Vietnamese catfish exports. In response, US producers successfully lobbied their government to change its food labelling rules, barring the Vietnamese exports from being labelled as catfish.

When this did not reduce imports, they successfully lobbied for the US government to initiate an anti-dumping investigation. As the bilateral trade agreement did not establish a mechanism for dispute settlement, the case was pursued in the US courts. Preliminary duties were imposed, reducing catfish imports from Vietnam by 30 to 40 per cent, and, after investigations, the US courts ruled in favour of the complainants.

The fact that Vietnam was not a WTO member undermined its leverage, as it could not appeal the decision through the WTO where the United States would have had to justify its measures on the basis of international standards. In the US domestic courts, Vietnam could not force the United States to take international standards into consideration, which enabled the US government to choose a standard to justify its policies. Furthermore, the WTO dispute settlement allows third parties to join the case, bolstering the legal arguments and legitimacy of the complaint. Vietnam did not have this option.

*Source*: Davis (2006).

## Influence the choice of venue, rules and procedures

Beyond choices over the negotiating forum, it is important to consider the rules of engagement and the extent to which these can be influenced. Seasoned negotiators express concern that negotiators often fall into a set of process choices without thinking through their implications.

A first factor to weigh up is whether negotiation is the best option. In instances where a dispute has arisen over the implementation of an existing agreement and litigation is an option, countries face the decision of whether to negotiate, litigate or, indeed, pursue both routes. While litigation is often perceived as a measure of last resort, negotiators suggest that it should be seen as a strategic move in a wider game of negotiation, and a particularly powerful way of bringing larger players to the table. Whether to negotiate or litigate was a decision developing countries faced when seeking to challenge the US cotton subsidies. In this instance, litigation was arguably the more effective route (see Case Study 8).

Smaller developing countries are, understandably, reluctant to pursue litigation against larger states, out of concern that it will be viewed as an act of hostility. However, the WTO dispute settlement mechanism offers the possibility for countries to join a case as co-complainants and as third parties, thus offering smaller countries the possibility of forging a coalition to bring about a case, which can help insulate them from political pressure.

---

**Influencing the venue, rules and procedures**

**Is there an option to litigate?** If so, when in the negotiating process should we take steps to litigate? What would the political ramifications be? Can we form a coalition of co-complainants?

**In which country should the negotiating meetings be held?** What would work to our greatest advantage?

**Can we influence the negotiating rules and procedures in our favour?** Who will chair? What are the decision-making processes?

---

Aside from large decisions such as whether to litigate, it is worth giving thought to smaller decisions such as the selection of venues for specific meetings. While these may appear to be immaterial, they can significantly influence the negotiating process. In the trade context, geographic considerations are often a significant factor, particularly for developing countries. If negotiations are held in a relatively remote location, it can be hard for smaller countries to finance the attendance of a full negotiating contingent. For this reason, many developing countries prefer to hold negotiating sessions in Geneva, where they have the logistical support of their missions.

In some cases, it may be possible for a developing country to offer to host a negotiating meeting. This can be advantageous as the negotiators from the host country are likely to have far more resources to hand, and they can exert a decisive influence over the logistical details of the negotiation such as planning the seating arrangements and the shape of the negotiating table. Even if a negotiating partner hosts the meeting, the small state can still turn this into an opportunity, by gathering intelligence on the interests and strategies of the host state, and meeting with potential allies within the host state (Bhuglah 2004).

In terms of specific rules and procedures, a number of recommendations emerge from past experience. Negotiations that are characterised by high levels of transparency generally work to the advantage of the weaker party, as when large powers know that their actions will come under public scrutiny, it is harder for them to breach the rules or resort to the use of coercive tactics. In the WTO, for instance, developing countries have lobbied for improved transparency and the adoption of guidelines to govern the composition of Green Room and other small group meetings (Deere Birkbeck 2011).

When there are many parties at the table, decisions might be made by a simple majority vote, by specified majority procedures (such as a 'qualified majority vote') or by full consensus. In the WTO, there has been substantial debate about whether the 'single undertaking' approach (nothing is agreed until everything is agreed) and decision-making by consensus should be abandoned in favour of agreements of partial scope and a process of majority voting. Many small developing countries oppose these proposals on the grounds that while the current approach is cumbersome, it does ensure that their issues are addressed, as (in theory at least) consensus voting provides them with veto power.

---

**Rules and procedures favouring small developing countries**

- Transparency;
- Consensual decision-making (providing small developing countries with veto power);
- Agreeing at the start to principles that the final outcome will further or respect (e.g. proportionality, development, food security).

---

Decisions over who will chair the negotiating session can be significant. The chairperson influences which participants speak and in what order, whether decisions will be made in sub-groups or plenary, how documents will be adopted and how they will be revised or amended. In the WTO, the large number of countries at the table and issues on the negotiating agenda has led to the practice of selecting a small group of 'friends of the chair' who facilitate negotiations in key issue areas. Although they are supposed to be impartial, there have been long-standing concerns among developing countries these 'friends' have been biased towards the interests of industrialised countries.

In the WTO context, small developing countries often have opportunities to serve as chairs of negotiating bodies, often because they are perceived as having little power and hence as being less likely to try and use the position of chair to further their own interests than large states. Chairing imposes some costs on small countries. The time demands are high and some of the ambassador's time and staff are diverted from pursuing their country's interests, they may miss meetings of other negotiating groups, and, when they attend a larger meeting, they may feel inhibited from taking strong positions on contentious issues. However, there are considerable benefits. Most obviously, the ambassador has much greater capacity to promote agreement than otherwise. In addition, chairing makes the small country more visible in the eyes of the WTO Secretariat and chairs of other bodies, hence more likely to be invited to informal meetings where key deals are hammered out. Attending such meetings gives a delegation special access to valuable political information about what others are doing throughout the round (Odell 2010: 562–563).

A final factor to consider is whether to advocate for the negotiations and their outcomes to be guided from the outset by a set of normative principles. In some negotiations, such principles can provide leverage to the weaker side. The inclusion of relatively innocuous-sounding commitments may be readily agreed to by larger states at early stages of the process, particularly if they reflect principles or objectives that have been agreed in other fora, and may provide a helpful reference point for later stages of negotiation. For instance, one might argue that the fact that all parties agreed that the Economic Partnership Agreement (EPA) negotiations would serve the development interests of African, Caribbean and Pacific (ACP) countries placed the European Union (EU) in the position of having to defend its actions against this benchmark and conferred additional legitimacy to concerns raised by ACP countries.

Aside from trying to influence the rules and procedures for a given negotiation, advocating for wider governance reforms can be in the long-term interest of developing countries. This is particularly true in an organisation like the WTO, which serves as a focal point for many negotiations. In advocating specific reforms, it is often helpful to justify proposals against some external or objective precedent based on a claim of fairness (Odell 2000; HBSP 2005; Narlikar 2006).

### Case Study 8: Negotiate or litigate? Tackling US cotton subsidises through the WTO

In the early 2000s, several developing countries became concerned that US cotton subsidies were depressing world prices, leading to unfair reductions in their income from cotton exports. While Brazil decided to pursue a litigation case via the WTO dispute settlement mechanism, Benin and the other three cotton-exporting African countries took a deliberate decision to take their concerns to the negotiating room. Even though they had the opportunity to sign on as co-complainants in the case brought by Brazil, they did not. They were concerned that litigation would take too long, that there would be adverse political ramifications and that, in the event of the United States failing to comply with a favourable ruling, they would be unable to effectively retaliate.

Although the African countries did manage to propel their concerns to the centre of the Doha Round negotiations, they were unable to secure a positive outcome, not least because their concerns were held hostage to the wider impasse in the negotiations. In contrast, Brazil won its initial case against the United States, as well as the subsequent appeals, and the WTO conferred on it the right to impose sanctions worth up to US$800 million by retaliating in goods and to cross-retaliate in intellectual property.

Using these decisions as leverage, Brazil was able to reach a settlement with the United States, under which the United States would finance technical assistance for Brazilian farmers (worth US$147 million annually), in return for being allowed to continue to subsidise its cotton production. In other words, the litigation case forced the United States to the table and enabled Brazil to secure some compensation. As a Brazilian deputy minister noted, 'Cases are a communication tool. They are an important instrument to make [the United States and the EU] sit down at the table and really negotiate seriously....'

As African countries were not party to the dispute, they were left 'on the sidelines' during the US–Brazil discussions, and the final settlement between these two parties did nothing to assuage their concerns: the settlement did not address the distortion of world cotton prices, and nor were African countries included in the US compensation package. Looking back, many argue that the African countries took the wrong choice. Had they signed on as co-complainants, they would have had a greater degree of success.

*Sources*: Charan Devereaux et al. (2006a) and ICTSD (2010).

## Time, structure and sequence negotiations carefully

For small developing countries, the timing, structuring and sequencing of a negotiation can have a significant impact on their ability to shape outcomes. In some cases, countries may be able to influence the timing of negotiations in their favour. The Republic of Korea, for instance, delayed bilateral trade negotiations over textiles with the United States until Taiwan and Singapore had completed similar negotiations. This revealed valuable information on the interests of the United States and their negotiating strategy, enabling Korea to ask for what the others had obtained and hold out for a little more (Odell 1985). Alternatively, countries may be able to delay negotiations until they have passed domestic legislation that helps to bind their negotiating position. It is much harder for a country to make a concession that requires overhauling domestic legislation, particularly if the issue is politically sensitive.

Countries can, in some instances, undertake pre-emptive policy actions that have a deterrent effect. For instance, one rationale for Mauritius enacting anti-dumping legislation and creating a specialised unit to investigate cases of dumping was the hope that this would act as a deterrent to countries that might otherwise seek to dump their exports on the Mauritian market, helping to avoid the need for Mauritius to pursue costly litigation to obtain redress.[1]

With regards to timing, experienced negotiators caution that negotiations can take several years to complete. They warn that inexperienced negotiators tend to feel bored, or feel concerned that they have not completed an agreement, which prompts them to press for completion when they shouldn't. Instead, negotiators can turn lengthy and drawn-out negotiations to their favour by using the delays to make effective moves away from table.

---

**Timing and sequencing**

Would it be advantageous to **wait and let others negotiate first?**

Is there a trade partner who might be more flexible, and with whom negotiations should be prioritised in order to set a **favourable precedent?**

What **target date** for completing negotiations is realistic?

Is it possible to introduce an **element of competition,** especially when negotiating with donors or foreign companies?

The structure and sequencing of negotiations can also have a bearing on the outcome. In many cases, developing countries only have a few specialised personnel, which means that officials typically have to cover several trade-related issue areas. In a complex negotiation such as a free trade agreement, it is often advantageous to advocate that working group sessions take place sequentially rather than in parallel. Sequential negotiation enables maximal participation, and provides sufficient time for negotiators to cope with the scope and depth of negotiating agenda (Bhuglah 2004; Echandi 2006).

In some situations, it may be possible to structure the negotiations in one's favour by introducing an element of competition into the negotiation, particularly when negotiating with donors or foreign investors. For instance, maximising competition among foreign investors bidding for oil concessions has helped Libya secure favourable terms (Case Study 9).

A similar lesson emerges from studies of aid negotiations. Since the early 2000s, donor countries have advocated that recipient governments negotiate with all donors at the same time to reduce transaction costs. However, this can greatly reduce the leverage of recipient countries as donors negotiate among themselves and then present a single offer to the recipient country, which is hard for the latter to influence. In contrast, holding a series of parallel one-on-one negotiations often provides recipient governments with greater leverage to shape aid programmes to meet their needs. Botswana, for instance, develops regular national development plans with specific projects and then negotiates with individual donors over the projects they are prepared to support. The government refuses aid that does not fit with its plan or if the project's recurrent costs cannot be managed, and it has insisted that donors specialise in specific areas. In this way, it has retained substantial control and ensured that the aid is directed in line with its national interests (Case Study 29).

---

**Case Study 9: Structuring negotiations for maximum advantage: Libya's oil auctions**

Despite its reliance on foreign oil companies for oil production, over the years Libya has proved its ability to impose tough fiscal terms. While structural factors have been favourable (Libya has a very strategic geographic location at the door of Europe and its oil fields have attractive geological characteristics) success is also attributable to Libya's deft negotiating strategy, particularly the way in which it structured negotiations with investors.

Libya's success started in the 1950s, when it introduced competition in the sector by limiting the size of single oil concessions to 75,000 km$^2$. The government succeeded in attracting major investors and a wide range of other smaller companies that had a few available upstream opportunities outside Libya, placing the Libyan government in a powerful bargaining position. In the years that followed, the government experimented with various initiatives to maximise its revenues from oil concessions, learning as it went. These included changing royalty levels, requiring varying levels of ownership by the national oil company and shifting the responsibility for pricing of oil from the companies to government. During some periods, the government set terms that were too harsh given the prevailing market conditions, deterring investors and pushing government to revise its policies.

In 2005, Libya held an oil auction that was particularly successful by world standards. The government followed new procedures with sealed-bid rounds, non-negotiable conditions, selection criteria (based on contractor share, exploration commitments, bonuses, parallel investment and local content), pre-qualification procedures and minimum expenditure commitment. A notable innovation was the decision to grant awards to companies that made the highest bid on the share of gross production going to the national oil company – this is a novelty as the share going to the national oil company is usually predetermined in the model contract or subject to negotiation. Following the auction, the average government income on concessions averaged more than 80 per cent, among the highest in the world.

*Source*: Fattouh and Darbouche (2010).

## Shape the agenda

Once the basic framework for the negotiation is set, it becomes important to think about how to influence the negotiating agenda. The agenda typically includes the list of topics and the sequence in which they will be addressed, and the amount of time scheduled for each item. The agenda determines whose views and interests are given priority and how the issues will be framed. By influencing which questions will be debated and in which order, a negotiator can bias the answers in his or her favour. In general, it is relatively easy to shape the agenda early on when the negotiating process is relatively fluid. It becomes harder as the negotiation progresses.

A first consideration for negotiators is whether there are issues that it is in their interest to see included or excluded from the negotiation, or linkages to other issue areas that it would be in their interest to propose or to block (Odell 2000: 205). For instance, linking negotiations to an issue area in which you have a strategic advantage may enhance your chances of success. In other instances, it may be critical for small developing countries to keep issues *off* the table, particularly if they do not have a thorough understanding of their interests in that area.

The decision to include or exclude an issue may differ across negotiations. For instance, Caribbean countries supported other developing countries in blocking negotiations over environmental and labour standards at the WTO, even though they were not 'red-line' issues for the Caribbean; they acted to avoid disunity within the developing country coalition. However, they took a strategic judgement to place these issues on the table during the EPAs on the basis that these issues were of great interest to the EU, and this would enable the Caribbean to obtain trade-offs in other areas.[2]

When considering the sequence in which issues will be addressed, some experts advise negotiators to start with issue areas where mutual concessions can be made and conclusion reached relatively quickly. This enables all parties to make gains at the start of the negotiation, fostering trust and laying a better foundation for the more challenging aspects of negotiation (Thompson 2012).

However, developing country negotiators content that the disadvantages of this approach can be substantial, and it is often more effective to negotiate on issues simultaneously. First, negotiating in sequence reduces the likelihood that negotiators will be able to create value by trading off across issue areas (this is discussed further in Chapter 4). Second, in the context of significant power asymmetry, it may be important for the weaker side *not* to make concessions until later on in the process, lest they be perceived as weak. In the North American Free Trade Agreement (NAFTA) negotiations on investment and energy supply commitments, for instance, Mexico adopted a hard defensive position until the last stage of the negotiations. Had it made concessions early on, the United States might well have pressed for further concessions (Ortiz Mena 2006).

---

**Shaping the agenda**

Which issues do we want to be **included or excluded?**

Are there **linkages** to other issue areas it would be advantageous to make or block?

How should issues be **sequenced** on the agenda? How many issue areas do we have the capacity to negotiate in parallel?

If our negotiating partner tables a **draft agenda**, or a **template agreement**, how will we respond?

---

A very common tactic used by stronger parties is to try and seize the negotiating initiative by presenting their negotiating partners with a completed agenda or even a fully drafted final agreement, to which the other party is asked to react. For instance, most bilateral investment treaties are negotiated on the basis of a 'model treaty' tabled by the stronger country. This immediately places the other party in a defensive position and, if the tactic is successful, the completed agenda or template agreement distracts the other party from focusing on their negotiating objectives and becomes a focal point around which the negotiations become centred.

To counter these effects, negotiators can try and pre-empt such moves by putting forward their own draft agendas or, if they are sufficiently prepared, a draft agreement. If the other party moves first, then they are advised to make a counterproposal as quickly as possible. The competing documents can then be used as the basis for forging a compromise (Salacuse 2000; Odell and Ortiz Mena 2004; Thompson 2012).

In practice, it may be very hard to influence a template text. Any deviation from the template is typically perceived as a hassle by large country negotiators, not only because such deviation can become a precedent for further negotiations but also because it may entail new consultations with domestic stakeholders (Echandi 2006). Negotiators may also use domestic politics as a negotiating tactic, saying, for instance, 'we cannot give this concession as it will have to go back to Congress and they will not approve' even when this is not the case. When faced with such an argument, it is valuable to know the internal domestic politics of the partner country in order to assess its credibility.

## Harness the power of coalitions and networks

Negotiators are unanimous in their opinion that forging or joining a coalition is one of the most valuable moves that a smaller side can make in a negotiation.

Negotiations in which there are many parties at the table are most amenable to coalition formation. In the trade context, this is particularly clear in WTO negotiations, where developing countries have greatly increased their leverage through the use of coalitions such as the G90, G33 and Least Developed Countries Group. Coalitions have also provided small developing countries with leverage in other trade negotiations (Narlikar 2003; Tussie and Saguier 2011). For instance, a united approach among ACP countries in the 1970s was crucial in helping them obtain concessions from Europe, including a shift from reciprocal to unilateral trade preferences and various Commodity Protocols under which Europe agreed to pay prices above the world average for exports such as bananas, sugar and rum.

*Forging or joining a coalition is one of the most valuable moves that a smaller side can make in a negotiation.*

Coalitions provide weaker parties with several distinct advantages. First, by acting together, states combine their limited resources, increasing the bargaining chips they can bring to the table and helping to offset power asymmetries. Second, the security of bargaining from a jointly held position can partially insulate small states from external pressures. Third, having a common negotiating platform allows countries to engage in joint capacity building as delegations can offset their individual technical resource constraints by sharing the organisational costs of negotiations and pooling technical expertise (Patel 2011). In negotiations where decisions are made by consensus, the formation of a coalition increases the credibility of threats to block agreements (Odell and Sell 2006).

Aside from formal coalitions, negotiators emphasise the need to build up informal networks in order to facilitate the exchange of information. Such networks are of obvious importance in Geneva, where they can help small delegations to obtain and share information about discussions in different negotiating groups and committees.

Networks among developing countries that are negotiating on a bilateral or regional level with a specific trading partner could offer significant advantages, yet their potential is often under-exploited. For instance, although developing countries all negotiate bilateral investment treaties with large industrialised countries, there are few strong informal networks that share information about how to negotiate these treaties most effectively. Similarly, an absence of strong informal networks among the six regional groupings of ACP countries during the EPA negotiations left them vulnerable to divide and rule tactics by the EU.

*How can developing countries use their participation in coalitions to best effect?* Studies suggest that the countries that are the most effective in harnessing the power of coalitions carefully identify which coalition will be most useful for pursuing their agenda at any one time. A key factor to consider is the extent to which coalition members share your country's interests. For instance, when Mauritius wanted to raise concerns over the erosion of preferences, it had to identify the most appropriate coalition. Although it was a member of the Africa Group, it was aware that countries from Northern Africa wanted to have greater access to the markets of industrialised countries, so they had no interest in defending existing preferences. In contrast, many members of the ACP Group were worried about preference erosion, so this was the most strategic group in which to advance this agenda.[3]

---

**Using coalitions for leverage**

**Which coalition** is likely to be most effective in this particular negotiation? Would it be advantageous to join or form an issue-based coalition? If so, who should be in it?

Should we offer to **lead** the coalition?

Can we improve the **internal management** of the coalition? Are there clear and effective mechanisms for decision-making, leadership selection and holding representatives to account?

Has the coalition **thoroughly prepared** for this negotiation? Do we have agreement on potential concessions and red-lines? Have we agreed on how to respond to divide and rule tactics?

---

Small developing countries tend to rely on regional and characteristic-based groupings. On the positive side, because members share a broad range of interests, such coalitions tend to be long lasting. This enables members to develop trust pool resources and develop systematic ways of working. Stability also enables coalitions to create shared institutions that can generate valuable information and technical expertise, which increases negotiating capacity. They also tend to be harder for others to break (Harvard Business Essentials 2005; Tussie and Saguier 2011).

Developing countries use issue-based coalitions to a lesser extent, although there is evidence that such coalitions can be very effective (Deere Birkbeck and Harbourd 2011). In issue-based coalitions, members form temporary alliances of convenience around single issues. Although they are more amenable to divide and rule tactics as there are fewer ties binding members, these coalitions are often more influential as members have a very specific common interest to focus on. For instance, issue-based coalitions enabled developing countries to obtain concessions on the use of positive and negative lists in the GATS (General Agreement on Trade in Services) negotiations, as well as the use of compulsory licensing in the TRIPS negotiations. Part of the explanation for success was that developing countries formed temporary alliances with some large industrialised countries (principally the EU) to argue against the positions taken by other industrialised countries (the United States in both instances) (Singh 2006). However, negotiators caution that forging an alliance with a large country is a step that requires utmost caution. Small developing countries report bitter experiences of entering into coalitions with larger states, only to find that the larger state has pursued its own interests at their expense.

While some argue that it is advantageous for small countries to lead coalitions, negotiators suggest that assuming leadership is a double-edged sword. Leadership roles can provide countries with access to inner-circle consultations, political prestige and additional material resources. However, to be effective, a leader cannot be seen to be partisan to their country's interests, so a small country may find that their national interests no longer receive as much attention.[4]

*How can the leverage of a coalition be maximised during a negotiation?*
To work effectively, coalitions need to have sound internal management. This includes clear principles for representation of coalition members, and mechanisms for internal transparency, institutionalised coordination and selection of leadership. Care needs to be taken to ensure that coalition representatives are accountable to their members, particularly where certain countries have more resources to devote to oversight of delegated representatives. Accountability guidelines should seek to ensure that representatives carefully listen to all views beforehand, follow the mandate given by the group, faithfully report back on

discussions and consult with interested members in a timely fashion (Deere Birkbeck and Harbourd 2011).

As with any negotiation, coalitions need to prepare thoroughly. Preparations include agreeing on concessions that the group would be prepared to make if necessary, the decision-making procedures that will be followed during negotiations, as well as the coalition's red-lines and 'walk-away' point. The experience of some countries suggests that coalitions should formalise such discussions into a collective negotiating mandate. Undertaking such a process has the benefit of ironing out differences between countries during the pre-negotiation phase, reducing the likelihood that the coalition breaks down during negotiations due to unresolved internal tensions. In the DR-CAFTA (Dominican Republic Central America Free Trade Agreement) negotiations, for instance, the failure of Central American countries to agree a formal mandate prior to negotiating with the United States left them vulnerable to divide and rule tactics, with the United States exploiting intra-regional differences (Carrion 2009).

In developing a joint mandate, it is particularly important to provide the appointed representative with sufficient scope to make some compromises in the negotiating room without returning to the whole membership for approval for every minor change in position, as this can greatly undermine the negotiating power of the coalition (without revealing the level of delegated authority to the other party as 'I must pause in order to consult' is an important tactic) (Deere Birkbeck and Harbourd 2011).

The size of a coalition can also affect its level of influence in the negotiating room, and there are several trade-offs to consider. In cases where a coalition seeks to exert leverage through threats to block consensus, coalitions need to be large enough to make their threats credible. However, large coalitions can be vulnerable to fragmentation in the face of 'divide and rule' strategies. To some extent, fragmentation can be averted through active diplomacy and side-payments within the group. In the TRIPS/health coalition, for instance, a core group of states were very active in persuading possible break-away factions to remain united with the coalition (Odell and Sell 2006).

Where coalitions of states seek to make arguments based on their identity such as being 'small and vulnerable', their arguments have greater weight and credibility when the majority of eligible states participate, and when all members of the group clearly meet the identity requirements. The 'small and vulnerable economy' coalition at the WTO, for instance, has faced the challenge of managing a trade-off between its size and the credibility of its arguments. Increasing the size of the group has increased its political voice, but the group has grown to include some countries that are not perceived to be particularly small, and some negotiators fear that this has undermined the legitimacy of its positions.[5] More generally, negotiators need to be aware that as the size of the coalition they join expands, it is less likely that the core interests of their country will be reflected in the group's position, as compromises have to be made in order to maintain the unity of the group.

The experience of the Africa Group in WTO negotiations provides valuable insights into how developing countries can sustain an effective coalition (Case Study 10).

### Case Study 10: Sustaining a coalition: lessons from the Africa Group in WTO negotiations

Coalitions are a crucial negotiating instrument, yet developing countries face sizeable difficulties in creating and sustaining cohesive forms of cooperation. These are particularly severe for African countries given their limited material and technical resources, political and economic reliance on donor aid, and structural dependence on preferential access to developed country markets. These attributes render coalitions vulnerable to defection in the face of external pressure.

Despite these challenges, and the faltering record of developing country coalitions, the Africa Group has emerged as a stable and strong coalition in WTO negotiations. The institutionalisation of rules, decision-making structures and communication channels both in Geneva and at the regional level appears to be a primary reason its durability. After its formation in 1999, the Africa Group met more frequently than any other WTO coalition. It developed an elaborate communication structure under the African Union, including plenary sessions, ad hoc working groups and various technical expert meetings, organised around regular conferences of African trade ministers. Significantly, these meetings included both Geneva-based negotiators and capital-based government officials and ministers.

These formal structures provided several advantages. Although the coalition was large, with over 40 members, regular meetings enabled countries to develop detailed understandings of each other's policy preferences and likely behaviour, and forge common negotiating positions. Formalising decision-making structures at the regional level introduced pressures on the group to consolidate its cooperation in Geneva and ensured a level of continuity and stability in the face of regular changes in government and the constant rotation of diplomats in Geneva. It also had repercussions at the domestic level: the systematic involvement of capital-based officials meant that the wider government was engaged and briefed, and this helped to keep WTO issues on the domestic political agenda.

Crucially, these structures made the coalition less vulnerable to external pressure. Historically, many developing country groups have fragmented due to a disjuncture between frontline negotiators and capital officials, which made coalitions vulnerable to outsiders selectively engaging capital-based officials to exploit divergences in their levels of understanding and political commitment to the collective. By ensuring that representatives from both Geneva and capitals were systematically involved, the Africa Group was able to reduce its vulnerability.

*Source*: Patel (2011).

## Forge alliances with the private sector and civil society

Aside from joining forces with other countries, negotiators from small developing countries can augment their leverage by forging alliances with non-state actors including business associations, consumer organisations, parliamentarians, civil society organisations, journalists, religious groups and think tanks. In an inter-state negotiation, alliances with non-state actors are particularly powerful if they cross national boundaries and include groups from within the domestic constituency of the parties across the negotiating table. Such alliances can exert valuable pressure on trading partners (Odell 2000; Laurent 2006; Tussie and Saguier 2011).

---

**Forging alliances**

*Potential allies*

- Companies from the target state with extensive trade or investment ties to your country;
- Sympathetic members of congress or parliament;
- Development NGOs;

- Consumer groups;
- Opinion leaders.

*Possible benefits of alliance*

- Exert political pressure from within target state;
- Act as a convener, opening up space for political lobbying;
- Bolster technical capacity (provision of information and analysis);
- Finance legal costs.

In forging cross-border alliances, small developing countries can be at an advantage, as the size and complexity of large states means they often have a multiplicity of interests and constituencies to manage and hold together. This unwieldiness creates opportunities that small developing countries can exploit (Salacuse 2000). When Peru challenged the EU's labelling practices (Case Study 7), for instance, its position was bolstered by the fact that it worked with a prominent UK consumer group. The United Kingdom purchased over 90 per cent of Peruvian sardine exports to the EU. A major UK consumer group wrote a letter in support of Peru's position which Peru attached to its submission to the WTO panel, and it was cited in the panel's report. This alliance was particularly effective as it undermined one of the EU's core arguments, namely that its position could be justified on the basis of consumer interests (Davis 2006: 235).

Establishing strategic alliances with non-state actors was a key factor in enabling Caribbean banana exporters to influence the outcome of negotiations between the EU and Latin American countries (Case Study 11).

### Case Study 11: Using coalitions, alliances and the media: Caribbean states and the 'banana wars'

The high-profile and long-running dispute over the EU's banana import regime was widely perceived as a straightforward dispute between the EU on one hand, and the US and Latin American exporters on the other. In reality, however, the dispute involved a diverse mix of participants, including several tiny 'Windward Island' states in the Eastern Caribbean: St Lucia, St Vincent, Dominica and Grenada. Bananas were a leading export for these small countries, and exports were heavily dependent on EU preferences.

Despite their size, during the 1990s, the Windward Islands decisively shaped Europe's banana import regime, ensuring that it retained its preferential character and that prices remained significantly above world market levels. While this was not sufficient to halt a decline in their exports, the islands, together with their allies and supporters, were successful in forestalling liberalisation. Several tactical moves helped the Windward Islands shape the outcome of the 'banana wars':

- Their diplomatic representatives to the EU clearly and consistently articulated their message. Crucially, their voices were joined by senior political figures including prime ministers who were visible and vocal campaigners in Brussels, London and Washington.
- They recognised that securing a favourable position in the European Council of Ministers (which had the decision-making authority) would require winning over public opinion and, to this end, they enlisted the support of various groups including the Commission, the EU Parliament, national governments and Parliaments, NGOs, church groups and journalists.
- They targeted important third parties, notably the United States, that were exerting pressure on Europe for liberal reform. This included lobbying the US Congress. Also, direct though limited contact was maintained with Latin American supplying states and the multinational companies themselves in the hope of at least tempering their opposition to a restrictive banana regime.
- They capitalised on the 'natural public sympathy for the underdog' and highlighted possible economic and social threats that liberalisation posed to the Windward Islands to provide their arguments with moral legitimacy, and this provided a rationale for the campaign.
- During the WTO dispute settlement process, the Windward Islands worked in coalition with other ACP producers; the ambassador of three of the Windward Islands chaired the ACP working group on bananas; and the group engaged the services of legal advisers who helped with the preparation of briefs.

*Source*: Laurent (2007).

Working with non-state actors can bolster negotiating capacity in different ways. A review of the literature reveals examples of alliances with private sector actors that have supported negotiators by directly providing information and analytical support, financing legal advice and lawyers in litigation cases. For instance, when Antigua took up a case against the United States over its GATS commitments in the WTO dispute settlement mechanism, the affected gambling companies provided vital sources of information and financial support; while close collaboration with the tuna industry helped Thailand successfully negotiate a new quota for tuna exports to the EU (Case Study 12).

In some instances civil society organisations have provided important technical capacity. In 2007, a British water company began an investor–state arbitration case against Tanzania. A coalition of five NGOs successfully petitioned the arbitration tribunal to accept their written submission. Their submission emphasised the public-interest nature of the case and brought sustainable development issues to the forefront. Two of the NGOs had been involved in an earlier, precedent-setting NAFTA arbitration and they brought deep legal expertise and arguably shifted the focus of the case.[6] The tribunal's final decision noted the usefulness of the NGO submission, and although Tanzania was found to have violated certain provisions of the relevant bilateral investment treaty, the investor was not awarded compensation. Tanzania's willingness to allow NGOs to participate in their arbitration arguably had a decisive impact on the outcome of the case.

While alliances with non-state actors can be crucial in helping to meet resource shortfalls, negotiators from small developing countries caution that there is the risk of the negotiating position of governments being unduly influenced or 'captured' by these groups. This risk is also present when donors provide negotiating support, a factor that is discussed in detail in Chapter 5. For this reason, it is important that small developing countries work to improve government capacity, reducing reliance on third parties, and, when support is solicited from third parties, to ensure that it is as insulated as possible from political influence.

---

**Case Study 12: Using alliances to bolster negotiating capacity: Antigua and Barbuda and Thailand**

*Antigua and Barbuda: foreign investors pay legal bills*

In 2003, Antigua and Barbuda initiated a dispute settlement case against the United States at the WTO. It became a landmark case, as it was only the second brought under the GATS agreement, and a tiny island won a case against one of the world's largest countries.

During the late 1990s, Antigua and Barbuda actively solicited investment by online gaming and other electronic commerce companies in a bid to generate employment and diversify the economy. The sector became a major employer, a major contributor to GDP and an important source of government revenue. When the United States banned credit card payments to Internet casinos, most of which are based overseas including in Antigua and Barbuda, the island state lodged a dispute case at the WTO.

After background research, Antigua's government officials were convinced they had a winnable case. 'Everybody who looked at it, including top lawyers and a former EU Commissioner on trade, said the case was solid.'[7] However, the cost of bringing the case was estimated at about US$2 million, a cost that the government could not afford. Discussions with the gaming companies eventually resulted in an agreement that the government would take on the case, if the – mostly British – owners of Antigua's gaming companies paid the legal fees directly. Despite US attempts to make the case as long and complex as possible, the alliance with the private companies enabled Antigua and Barbuda to afford legal representation throughout the dispute settlement process, which it eventually won (although the United States subsequently refused to adhere to the ruling).

*Thailand: private sector provides information, negotiating support and finances legal counsel*

Between 2000 and 2003, Thailand, the world's largest exporter of canned tuna, successfully challenged the EU's preferential import regime for tuna. The scheme favoured exporters from ACP countries, and as this violated WTO rules on non-discrimination, the EU needed a WTO waiver. Threatening to block a waiver, the Thai government forced the EU into a consultation and formal mediation process, the result of which was an agreement to provide an annual tariff rate quota of 13,000 tonnes at 12 per cent for Thai tuna (compared with the standard tariff of 24 per cent).

Close collaboration with the tuna industry was a critical factor in Thailand's success. From the initial consultation process through to the final conclusion of the agreement, the Thai Tuna Packers' Group and the Ministry of Commerce worked in close partnership. Representatives from the private sector were present at consultations and negotiations to provide industry data and other factual evidence to support the government's arguments, and the tuna industry pooled its resources and hired a Brussels-based international law firm to provide additional legal support to the government negotiators.

*Source*: Antigua and Barbuda (Interview with negotiator, September 2008) and Thailand (Xuto 2005).

## Use high-level political lobbying to expand negotiating space

Intervention by high-level politicians is a tactic commonly used by both industrialised and developing countries. As one developing country negotiator observes, 'when we are right technically or legally, the other side proposes to move the discussion to the political level'.[8]

Developing countries have used intervention from their most senior politicians to help get issues onto the negotiating table and to increase the leverage of their country inside the negotiating room (Case Study 13). For instance, the intervention of the president of Burkina Faso, the first head of state to ever address the WTO General Assembly, was a decisive moment that helped propel cotton subsidies to the centre of the Doha Round.

Political leaders can enter into informal dialogue with their counterparts and, where relevant, key stakeholders in the target country. Such lobbying can help developing countries to gather intelligence on the interests of other negotiating parties, and, crucially, it provides them with an opportunity to convince political leaders from larger countries to support them *in principle*. As a WTO negotiator from a small state explained, 'To influence in Geneva you need to make use of political processes outside Geneva' (Jones et al. 2010: 56).

---

**Using high-level political lobbying**

**Which people or institutions are we seeking to influence?** Who are the key decision-makers that we need to influence?

> **What type of message or information** are they most likely to respond to?
>
> **Who should be the messenger?** Our president? Minister? Who are they most likely to listen to?
>
> **Who should accompany the principal messenger?** Are there allies from within the other country whose presence might add weight and credibility to our message?

Several considerations need to be made when planning a lobbying round. After identifying the individuals and organisations that need to be influenced, it is important to reflect on the type of message or information that the person or organisation is most likely to respond to, and the messenger that they are most likely to listen to. In many cases, it may be helpful to form alliances with powerful groups within the target country. In terms of messaging, industrial groups are likely to be receptive to arguments focused on their business interests; NGOs, parliamentarians and officials from development ministries, to arguments focused on public interest, poverty and development; while foreign ministers and heads of state, are likely to be most receptive to arguments focused on security implications (Insanally 2011).

In asking their political leaders to step in, negotiators need to carefully weigh up the political signal they are sending to the other party. In particular, if small countries convey the impression that they are desperate for agreement, this can reduce their leverage. For instance, one senior negotiator expressed concern that in negotiations with the EU, the position of the Caribbean had been weakened when, instead of sending a single spokesperson, 14 heads of state went to meet with the president of the European Commission (Jones et al. 2010: 66).

> **Case Study 13: Calling on the executive: Mauritius, Burkina Faso and Guyana**
>
> *Mauritius*
>
> In Mauritius, strong executive commitment to trade negotiations has produced results. Prime ministers have engaged other heads of state in direct dialogue, including the former French president on the EU Sugar Regime and the US president on the African Growth and Opportunity Act (AGOA). When the EU

announced compensation for ACP sugar producers affected by a one-third reduction in guaranteed sugar prices, the Mauritian government was dissatisfied with its share of the compensation. The prime minster directly lobbied the EU and succeeded in augmenting the Mauritian share of the compensation from 15 to 18 per cent.

### Burkina Faso

The African Cotton Initiative similarly had full and consistent political support at the highest level in all four countries involved. The intervention of President Blaise Compaoré of Burkina Faso was decisive in putting cotton onto the agenda of the Doha negotiations. In 2003, he delivered a resounding speech at the WTO general assembly asking for the implementation of Doha commitments and arguing that the damage done by subsidies to West African economies amounted to more than all the aid they received. This speech 'changed everything overnight'. It shifted public opinion and galvanised the support of many WTO member states. This placed pressure on the WTO secretariat to put cotton on the negotiating agenda, scheduling it for the first day of the negotiations, and, in a highly unconventional move, the Secretary General of the WTO chaired the negotiating session, imploring member states to take the African cotton proposal seriously (although to date the African countries have not obtained concrete policy changes).

### Guyana

In the late 2000s, in the context of international climate change negotiations, President Jagdeo of Guyana took up the challenge of getting an agreement on an international award system for avoided deforestation. The president became a prominent interlocutor for this issue on the international stage, and Guyana, together with Gabon, was invited to join G20 discussions on deforestation. This helped to galvanise support for the issue and generated significant commitments from other countries for resources to support Guyana's initiatives.

*Sources*: Jones et al. (2010) and Trotz (2011).

## Use the media

Public opinion, typically mediated through media coverage, can play a decisive role in negotiations, shaping countries' negotiating objectives. In many countries the media influences the policy agenda: media coverage has the power to force items onto the agenda and, in many cases, to order the priorities for debate. In the words of one distinguished international relations professor, 'The world of traditional power politics was typically about whose military or economy wins, but in an information age, power is also about whose story wins.... Narratives become the currency of soft or attractive power' (Nye 2010). In many instances, public opinion is sympathetic to the 'underdog', and so obtaining coverage in the media can be a powerful way for the smaller party in a negotiation to obtain leverage.

Getting an issue favourably covered in the media requires careful planning. A first step is to identify the target audience and hence the media outlet that is most suitable. For instance, if the objective is to put public pressure on senior politicians from the counterparty, then obtaining widespread coverage in their national newspapers is extremely useful. In other cases, the objective may be to raise awareness among the political decision-makers from a wide range of countries, in which case the more specialised international economic and business media might be more appropriate. This may include the *Financial Times*, *The Economist* and wires such as Reuters and the Inter Press Service.

A particular challenge for trade negotiators is to turn their negotiating objectives into a story that the press are eager to cover. Compelling stories sell papers, and these are what journalists need. There are two criteria for deciding what makes a good story: currency (an issue has to be alive and related to happenings and events) and reader interest. In general, the types of qualities that good news stories possess are similar to those of popular fiction: drama, emotion and a strong, simple plot (Lattimer 2000).

---

**Securing media coverage**

**What is my target audience**, and what is the best media outlet for reaching it?

**Is there a clear and compelling storyline?** Is there a human face?

**How can we ensure the proposed story has currency?** Is it linked to an event or burning national or international issue? Is it possible to generate interest in the issue by launching a report, exposing the negotiating tactics of the other side, a letter to the editor, a stunt?

**Is it possible to enlist the support of media-savvy groups** that can help develop and pitch the story? Should we engage the services of a professional PR agency?

Major ministerial meetings, pivotal moments in a negotiation, or significant trade policy decisions can often provide currency. It may also be possible to generate coverage around the launch of a report, leaking or exposing the negotiating practices of the other side, or through a letter to the editor from leading personalities. During the EPA negotiations between ACP countries and the EU, for instance, one story that received international coverage was that the Pacific Islands threatened to walk out of negotiations, accusing the EU of tying aid to market opening. The story appears to have been leaked by the Pacific negotiators to the press in a bid to diffuse the potential threat. Coverage in the international media prompted the EU to issue a swift rejoinder, apparently having the intended effect (Bounds 2007).

When courting the media, it is helpful to identify a clear, compelling angle and to link the story to a human face, so journalists can follow-up with interviews. The concerns of the cotton-exporting African countries received a high level of coverage because their arguments against US subsidies could readily be told as a story of David versus Goliath, pitting poor West African smallholders against the heavily subsidised American industrial farmers. It could also be used to highlight the hypocrisy in US advocacy for free trade. The African countries worked with media-savvy NGOs to pitch their stories, with great success. In the United States, major papers ran several stories and editorials backing the African countries, including the *New York Times* and the *Wall Street Journal* (Heinisch 2006).

In mounting a media campaign, it may be useful to enlist the support or services of public relations professionals (Case Study 14).

**Case Study 14: Mounting a media campaign: the experience of Caribbean sugar-exporting countries**

In 2004, the EU announced a dramatic reform of its sugar regime, with significant implications for ACP sugar exporters. The guaranteed sugar prices that these countries received in the EU market under the EU–ACP Sugar Protocol would be cut by 39 per cent over three years, beginning in 2005. Despite the sizable negative economic and social implications for these countries, there was no offer of compensation, and only vague promises of 'accompanying measures' to help them adjust their production systems. In response, the Caribbean sugar exporters, together with other affected ACP countries and industry and NGO allies in Europe, mounted a campaign to persuade the EU to modify its reform proposals.

Caribbean heads of state, ministers and affected companies undertook a series of lobby meetings with key decision-makers in Europe. However, it soon became clear that this would not be sufficient to influence the reforms. Ministers decided to invest in an EU-wide media campaign in the hope of galvanising popular support for their positions, which, they hoped, would influence European decision-makers. They appointed a public relations company to run a media campaign, funded by the Caribbean sugar companies. The company ran press conferences, cultivated a network of high-profile journalists across the EU, pitched stories, produced a series of communications materials and arranged high-profile interviews. From being a peripheral concern in the debate over EU sugar reforms, the impact on ACP countries became a central feature of the media coverage.

Ultimately, ACP countries were unable to significantly alter the reform proposals, but they were able to secure additional funds for 'accompanying measures' to support adjustment to a liberalised market. Cultivating sympathy among the European public arguably helped the Caribbean to obtain this outcome.

*Source*: Insanally (2011).

Media stunts, where a visually captivating display is created to provide journalists with photo and video coverage to accompany reports, are commonly used by NGOs but rarely by governments. A recent creative stunt involving the president and cabinet of the Maldives is a notable exception. It received worldwide media attention and dramatically increased the public profile of the small island state (Case Study 15).

> **Case Study 15: Captivating the media: the Maldives and climate change negotiations**
>
> The Maldives is a small country that is extremely vulnerable to climate change. During the late 2000s, the president took a series of steps to propel his country to the forefront of global negotiations on climate change. One of the most successful steps was a publicity stunt where the president held a cabinet meeting 4 metres underwater, two months ahead of the Copenhagen climate negotiations. The visually striking stunt captivated the world's media, becoming one of the most widely used images throughout the ensuing negotiation, and it helped the president of the Maldives secure high-profile interviews with the major international media.
>
> Having found ways to secure media attention, the challenge for the Maldives was to use this attention to induce change in the negotiating positions of other countries. A major impediment to securing commitments from industrialised and large developing countries is the argument that mitigation is too expensive and impractical. To help refute this argument, the Maldives has taken the lead in mitigation commitments. It was the first country to sign up to the Kyoto Protocol, and in 2009 it set itself the task of becoming the first carbon-neutral country in the world. These moves were particularly notable given that it is a relatively poor developing country. Whether these measures succeed in influencing the policies of other countries remains to be seen.
>
> *Source*: Lang (2009).

## Actively manage domestic politics

While the primary focus of negotiators is the party across the table, political mobilisation within one's own country can have a decisive impact on the outcome of a negotiation. As one expert notes, 'If negotiators take the domestic political landscape for granted, they can step on a landmine' (Odell 2000: 216).

Negotiators need to think through the repercussions of their negotiating strategy on domestic constituencies and proactively manage these relationships. If, for instance, a government anticipates that it will have to make specific concessions in order to obtain a particular agreement, it is important to enter into an early discussion with stakeholders that stand to lose. Alternatively, if negotiators wish to issue a threat such as walking away from the negotiations, it is crucial that strong domestic opposition to going ahead with that threat does not undermine its credibility. More generally, negotiators need to be aware that garnering a high level of public support for a particular initial negotiating position can make it extremely difficult for them to subsequently back down or make concessions (Odell 2000: 216–217). While this is often a disadvantage, galvanising a high level of public support around a country's 'red-lines' can help it to hold strong in the negotiating room.

---

**Actively manage domestic politics**

**Which groups are potentially influential?** Have those with the potential to block the deal, as well as all potential allies been identified?

**Have negotiations with those who must approve and implement the deal been anticipated?**

**Are there particular 'red-line' issues around where strong public support would strengthen our negotiating hand?**

**Are there areas where we want to make concessions but there is likely to be strong opposition from influential groups?** How might this be diffused?

---

Experience shows that shaping the perceptions of domestic stakeholders, particularly the broader public, takes time and requires repeated explanation and argumentation. Moreover, it is crucial to distil complex trade issues into clearly articulated and simply expressed goals in order to capture the public imagination (Laurent 2006). A deliberate public outreach strategy can be helpful, involving regular press briefings, press releases, op-eds and forging alliances with NGOs. Cultivating a group of friendly journalists and public opinion leaders can help ensure that a particular argument is widely heard.

For stakeholders that are particularly powerful and opposed to the government's negotiating position, it may be possible to bring them on board if a minister or high-ranking official contacts them personally to impress upon them the importance of the negotiating position for the country. A proactive media campaign about the benefits of a particular negotiating position for other sectors of society can also help to dilute the influence of large players (Mo 2004).

In thinking through the domestic political angle of a negotiation, a negotiator should ideally map out all the interested parties (those with a stake in the outcome) and think through the ways in which they could affect the negotiating process. On this basis, decisions can be made about how and when to involve them in the negotiating process. A series of questions can aid this mapping process: Who might value this deal the most, and are they at the table or otherwise involved? Have all the potentially influential players been identified? Have those with the potential to block the deal, as well as all potential allies, been identified? Have negotiations with those who must approve and implement the deal been anticipated? (Lax and Sebenius 2006).

Analysis of Costa Rica's national referendum on DR-CAFTA illustrates the ways in which trade negotiations can become highly politicised in the domestic setting (Case Study 16).

---

**Case Study 16: Influencing public perceptions: the politics of the DR-CAFTA referendum in Costa Rica**

In October 2007, Costa Rica became the first developing country to hold a public referendum on an international trade agreement. The referendum asked voters to decide whether or not the country should enter into DR-CAFTA, a free trade agreement between five Central American countries (Costa Rica, El Salvador, Guatemala, Honduras and Nicaragua), the Dominican Republic and the United States. The referendum passed with a wafer-thin margin: 52 per cent voted for the agreement, and 48 per cent against.

The debate during the lead-up to the referendum was highly salient and politicised. Costa Rica, along with the other countries involved, had signed the DR-CAFTA agreement in 2004. However, while the others had gone ahead to ratify it, the timing of elections in Costa Rica combined with a high level of popular opposition had delayed ratification, and the government eventually called a national referendum. While the government and large industries were strongly in favour of the agreement, a large social movement, including labour unions, students and religious groups, vigorously opposed it.

Ultimately, the government was able to sway a sufficiently high level of voters to back its negotiating position. This appears to have been largely attributable to the strength and resources of the well-established political party (the PLN (Partido Liberación Nacional)) that backed it. Although the anti-CAFTA 'No' campaign had undertaken extensive analysis, developed sophisticated arguments against the agreement and had a high level of grassroots support, it had to rely largely on word of mouth to convey its message and its networks were limited to the urban areas. In contrast, the government and its pro-CAFTA 'Yes' campaign had the resources to embark on a mass media campaign and it was able to use the resources and established political networks of the PLN, which spanned both urban and rural areas. For instance, the 'Yes' campaign contracted a public relations company to help convey its messages, set up a network of 'information centres' in rural areas, and used over 20,000 vehicles to transport its supporters to polling stations. There were also suggestions that mayors in the rural areas had been placed under a high level of political pressure to support the 'Yes' campaign.

*Sources*: Sánchez-Ancochea (2008) and Hicks et al. (2011).

## Summary

This chapter has explored the moves that negotiators can make 'away from the table'. It has shown that many of the important decisions that affect outcomes are taken either before the parties sit down at the table or away from the table once negotiations are underway. It has highlighted the need to pay attention to decisions over where the negotiation takes place; the negotiating rules and procedures that will be followed; and the way the agenda is structured. Once formal negotiations have started, it has underscored the value of continuing to make moves away from the table, including forging strategic coalitions with other countries and alliances with non-state actors; engaging in high-level lobbying; influencing public opinion, particularly through the media; and actively managing relationships with domestic constituents.

In the next chapter, we turn to examine other types of tactical moves, namely those made at the negotiating table.

**Checklist: Moves Away from the Negotiating Table**

**Which forum?** Should we negotiate at the WTO, regionally or bilaterally? Should we try to exclude any party? Should we keep negotiating or initiate dispute settlement?

**Would timing or sequencing make a difference?** Can we influence the rules and procedures to work in our favour?

**Who should be at the table?** Should we negotiate alone or in a group? Who is our best spokesperson? Who should be in our delegation?

**What issues should be included and excluded, if possible?** What linkages should be proposed or blocked?

**Which countries and interest groups can we ally with who would put pressure on the other party?**

**Can we shape public opinion in our favour?**

**Would intervention by our head of state open up negotiating space?**

**Are we successfully managing internal political debates?**

# 4
# Moves at the Negotiating Table

Once the negotiation has been thoroughly analysed, and the set-up is decided, the more formal stage of negotiating starts.

This chapter examines the moves that negotiators can make 'at the table' in order to maximise their influence over outcomes. It explores the ways in which negotiators can both create value in a negotiation to maximise the value on the table, and claim value in order to maximise their party's share of the gains when this value is distributed. It then looks in greater depth at the tactics that are especially relevant to trade negotiations: persuading the other party through the use of framing and fact-based arguments; using personal behaviours and qualities to influence the process in your favour; effectively negotiating across cultures; and using and responding to pressure tactics.

## Moves to create value

Getting a good deal in a negotiation is not simply about claiming as much value as you can. Negotiation texts emphasise that a much more important, and difficult, task is to create additional value. Alternatively put, it is smart to increase the "size of the pie", so that there is ultimately more "pie" on the table to divide.

To see the merit in this argument, it is helpful to think through three types of value-creating agreement. The first, and most obvious, occurs when the parties want a similar outcome or face similar problems, and where a solution would provide unequivocal gains to everyone. Imagine a situation where there was no rule on which side of the road cars should drive on, resulting in chaos, traffic jams and numerous accidents. Negotiating a rule would result in unequivocal gains to all parties, regardless of whether the decision was that cars would drive on the left or right side.

A second type of value-creating agreement arises when underlying interests are entirely complementary, even though this might not be seen at first. The classic example in the literature is of two sisters who are arguing over a single orange, an argument that looks at first glance to be a straightforward zero-sum or 'win-lose' negotiation. However, probing the reasons why they want the orange reveals differences – one sister wants the flesh to make juice, the other wants the peel as a cooking ingredient. By agreeing that one sister will get the flesh, and the other the peel, they are both left better off. As two experts note, in many cases, 'behind opposed positions lie shared and compatible interests, as well as conflicting ones' (Fisher and Ury 1991).

The third type of value-creating agreement, which is least intuitive yet arguably most relevant to more complex negotiations, creates value by exploiting the differences in the ways that parties prioritise issues. When there is more than one issue in a negotiation, which is the case with most trade negotiations, then the probability that negotiators will have identical preferences across all of them is small, and differences in preferences, beliefs and capacities can be traded off for joint gain. The key to creating value in such situations is finding 'complementary differences' – concessions that are relatively easy for one party to make, yet are valued relatively highly by the other side.

Creating new value is not a matter of altruism or kindness: it offers an opportunity to capture a portion of it. In other words, 'if the other party values something more than you do, let them have it – but don't give it away, sell it' (Malhotra and Bazerman 2007: 61).

*What tactics can negotiators use to create joint value?* The key to creating value is to maximise the number of 'tradable' issues on the negotiating table at any one time. This can be aided by unpacking issues into their component parts, introducing new issue areas, or dropping or de-linking contentious issues from the negotiations.

---

**Creating value**

Does the negotiation contain **more than one issue?**

Can **other issues** be brought in? Can issues be unbundled? New issues created?

Can **side deals** be made?

Do parties have **different preferences** across negotiation issues?

Are the **distributional implications** (the expected gains and losses) clear or disputed? If they are disputed, is it possible to use a **contingent contract** to reach agreement?

Another tactic is to probe behind negotiating positions to understand the underlying interests and discover differences, and then trade these differences. This process is often referred to as 'logrolling'. It relies on developing an inventory of all the ways in which you differ from your counterparts, and using those differences as ingredients for joint gains. To identify such areas, it helps to ask, 'what is something that they want badly, and which we do not value nearly as much?' (Lax and Sebenius 2006: 123). To facilitate logrolling during the negotiation it is helpful to negotiate multiple issues simultaneously, rather than sequentially; to make package offers that propose trade-offs across issue areas; and to ensure that a final agreement on any single issue is not reached until every issue has been discussed.

Differing beliefs among the negotiating parties, particularly about the future, are a frequent obstacle to reaching value-creating agreements. For instance, in a trade negotiation, the parties may have conflicting beliefs about the likely welfare gains that will accrue to each party from a given trade liberalisation scenario. In some instances, new research, commissioned jointly or separately, may provide information that helps to reduce initial uncertainty and open parties' eyes to unsuspected opportunities for creating value (Odell 2000: 212).

However, introducing new information is not always sufficient for overcoming such differences, especially if each side is confident about the accuracy of his or her predictions and consequently suspicious of the other side's forecasts, or when there is no consensus about the right method for analysing information. The accuracy of models is a particular challenge for trade negotiations, where computable general and partial equilibrium models are commonly used to estimate the gains that will accrue to each party. This method of analysis has been widely criticised, and even those who agree with the broad approach note that such models are only as accurate as the assumptions that underpin them.

The use of models during the Doha Round provides a good illustration of their limits. Proponents of the negotiations used such models to argue that trade liberalisation would lead to high gains, particularly for developing countries. In 2006, a new model was developed by the Carnegie Endowment, which followed the same method but used different assumptions (crucially, it did not rely on the assumption that there is full employment in developing countries). The results were striking and starkly different from the received wisdom. They suggested that any of the plausible trade scenarios in the Doha Round would produce only modest gains for the world; the liberalisation of agricultural trade would not be a panacea for most poor countries; the poorest countries might actually lose from any agreement; and additional special measures would be needed to ensure that the least developed countries succeed (Polaski 2006).

When the facts of a case are unclear or contested, compromise is unlikely to be a viable solution; each party may be reluctant to change his or her point of view, and different interpretations of the facts of a situation may threaten already tenuous relations. Contingent contracts can provide a way out of the mire. Rather than try and bridge differences of opinion between negotiators, they become the core of the agreement. Negotiations in the 1970s over the Law of the Sea are a powerful of how a contingent contract can be structured to create value in situations where the interests of the parties appeared irreconcilable (Case Study 17).

While contingency contracts can be a powerful tool for creating value, they are not always desirable. There are several caveats to bear in mind. First, they are risky if the other party is more knowledgeable than you. Second, they are useful only if uncertainty will be resolved in ways that can be measured objectively, so that they can be enforced. Parties need to agree upfront on clear, specific measures concerning how the contract will be evaluated. To ensure the contract can be objectively interpreted, it may be wise to consult a third party when drafting the contract (Thompson 2012: 210–211). Finally, it is important to think through the likely effect of the contingency contract on the incentives of the other party; the terms of the contract should provide incentives for the other party to behave in ways that are compatible with the spirit of the agreement (Malhotra and Bazerman 2007: 71).

---

**Case Study 17: Creating value: contingent contracts in law of the sea negotiations**

In 1973, the third UN Conference on the Law of the Sea was convened, with the ambitious objective of creating a new comprehensive law that would be internationally accepted. By 1978, agreement had been reached on 90 per cent of the issues, but positions on the remaining 10 per cent were so divergent that agreement seemed impossible. Deep-sea mining was one of the most intractable issues.

After two years of intense negotiations, agreement was finally reached on deep-sea mining. Success was largely attributed to skilful mediation by Singapore's ambassador Tommy Koh, who created a new process to shift parties' attention from defending their antagonistic positions to learning new information. He facilitated the creation of a contingent contract that dovetailed the differences in preferences between richer and poorer countries into a deal that each group considered a gain.

One major source of difference was that developing countries anticipated that seabed mining would be extremely profitable, while developed countries (whose companies were mining the seabed) argued that the returns would be modest. This made it impossible for the parties to agree on a single arrangement for taxation and profit sharing. New research and analysis failed to shift these positions, but it did help to clarify differences in opinions. A two-tier arrangement was negotiated whereby low-success mining projects would pay low royalties and profit shares, while high-success projects would pay high royalties and profit shares.

A second major source of difference was between companies, who had to invest heavily and wanted low tax rates to increase the odds of recouping their upfront investment, and the international community, who sought to maximise their revenue stream. Again, it was possible to dovetail differences through the use of a contingent contract: mining companies would pay lower levels of tax during the period when they were recouping their investments, and higher levels of tax later on in the process when investment and interest charges had been recovered.

*Sources*: Sebenius (1984) and Odell (1999).

Two further pieces of advice that negotiating textbooks advocate for creating value in a negotiation is to 'negotiate from interests rather than positions' and to 'separate the people from the problem'. While these are generic to all negotiations, they are worth briefly discussing.

Negotiations often fail or falter because negotiators get stuck defending positions, rather than focusing on the interests that lie behind them. The more a negotiator clarifies his or her position and defends it from attack, the more committed they become to it. Their ego becomes identified with their position, creating a situation where the negotiator has a new interest in 'saving face', making compromise less and less feasible, even when this would be in the interest of both sides (Fisher and Ury 1991: 3–8).

Psychology studies show that positional bargaining often occurs because partisans for one side tend to exaggerate the incompatibility of the two sides' goals, failing to see opportunities for mutual gain that a neutral observer might perceive (Odell 2000: 214). This is particularly likely to happen if negotiators are inadequately prepared. In the absence of clarity over their own interests, negotiators frequently adopt the non-strategy of simply opposing any position that the other party takes.

In many instances, negotiations become tangled up in the personalities at the table and the personal relationships between the negotiators rather than focusing on the objective merits of the problem. In some cases, a deeply adversarial relationship develops that derails the negotiations, particularly if negotiator egos become caught up in the process. In other cases, the personal relationship between the negotiators becomes too close, and this poses the risk that the negotiator accepts an unfavourable deal in order to preserve their personal relationship with the other side.

## Moves to claim value

Ultimately, any value created during a negotiation has to be split at some point, so effective distributive or value-claiming tactics are a vital part of the negotiator's repertoire. Narrowly speaking to maximise their share of the value, the negotiator is looking to reach an outcome that is just above the other party's walk-away point, so it is just attractive enough to induce the other party to agree, while allowing the focal negotiator to reap as much of the gain as possible (Thompson 2012: 61).

When negotiating with a far larger party, a primary challenge for the smaller party is to defend themselves against value-claiming tactics. At some stage in most trade negotiations, smaller countries find themselves on the receiving end of aggressive value-claiming tactics from larger countries. These include opening with high demands, refusing all concessions, exaggerating one's minimum needs and true priorities, manipulating information to others' disadvantage, worsening their alternative to an agreement, filing a legal complaint, making threats and actually imposing penalties (Odell and Ortiz Mena 2004: 5). In such situations, larger states have the upper hand by virtue of their larger market size, greater resources and, in many cases, stronger alternative options.

A common move for claiming as much value as possible is to make the first offer. The primary benefit is that it serves as an anchor, focusing the other party's attention and expectations. Particularly if the other party is unclear as to what is the correct, fair or appropriate outcome, they are likely to gravitate towards the first offer and use this as their reference point for the rest of the negotiations. Whether it is wise to make the first offer depends on the reliability of information a negotiator has, particularly about the other party's walk-away point. Making the first offer when such information is weak can be extremely costly. For instance, if a negotiator thinks that the other party's BATNA is stronger than it really is, they might make a first offer that is more 'generous' than it needs to be, thereby giving up substantial value. Alternatively, if they think their BATNA is weaker than it really is, they may table a first offer that is far too aggressive, running the risk that they will walk out.

---

**Claiming value**

**Have I made every effort to discover the other party's BATNA?** Have I exhausted all pre-negotiation sources of information? What assumptions am I making about their BATNA? Have I asked indirect questions to challenge these assumptions and to try and ascertain their walk-away point?

**Is my information about their walk-away point *so reliable* that it would be strategic to make the first offer?** Or, should I wait for them to make the first move?

**Am I defending myself against their attempts to anchor the negotiation?**

**Am I haggling effectively?** Am I avoiding unilateral concessions? Am I asking for proportionate concessions?

---

In general, if you have extremely reliable information, it is worth opening with a sufficiently aggressive offer that will anchor the negotiation in your favour. However, if you have little information, it is usually wise to wait, and let the other party make the first offer, not least because this may reveal information about their aspirations and walk-away point (Malhotra and Bazerman 2007: 30).

*How should you respond to the other party's offer?* When the other party makes the first offer, it is important to defend yourself against being influenced by their attempt to anchor. A crucial line of defence is to separate 'information' from 'influence'. The best way to stave off influence is to stick to the original game plan. If you began the negotiation with a prepared first offer, then only adjust it if the other party has provided credible information that changes your beliefs about their walk-away point – do not allow the other side's anchor to soften your first offer. Beyond this, it is important to avoid dwelling on the other party's anchor, as the more an anchor is discussed, the more powerful it becomes as a reference point (Malhotra and Bazerman 2007: 31–33). A negotiator's objective should be to re-anchor the negotiation in their favour as quickly as possible.

At some stage, negotiations often enter a period of haggling in order to reach a final agreement. There are several tips for effective haggling. First, focus on the other party's BATNA, rather than your own, thereby setting high aspirations. Second, avoid making unilateral concessions: only make concessions when the other party reciprocates. For this, it is important to be comfortable with silence. A particularly risky time to speak is if you have made an offer and the other party is considering it. All too often, if the other party is taking time to respond, negotiators get nervous and make further concessions. Third, make it clear what you expect from the other party in return: explain the costs attached to your concession, and ask for a concession that is proportionate in value (Malhotra and Bazerman 2007: 42–45).

## Overcome the 'negotiator's dilemma'

Ideally, negotiators should aim to create as much joint value as possible (maximise the size of the pie) and claim as much value as possible for their party (maximise the size of their slice). Yet while creating value requires sharing information and hence communication, trust, openness and creativity, these are the very qualities that can leave a negotiator vulnerable to exploitation in the distributive moments of the negotiation. The negotiating literature refers to this tension as the 'negotiator's dilemma'.

The negotiator's dilemma is particularly acute for developing countries that are negotiating with larger countries. Given their vulnerability to exploitation, how might a relatively small country help ensure that an agreement creates as much value as possible, while defending itself effectively against exploitative behaviour from larger states?

Three pieces of advice stand out. The first is to find out as much about the other party as possible: 'ask, listen, and learn'. Asking open-ended questions and listening attentively helps elicit information about underlying interests and facilitates the identification of areas where differences might make it possible to create value. In addition, carefully structured questions may elicit valuable information about the other party's alternatives and walk-away point (Lax and Sebenius 2006: 207).

The second is to 'divulge information strategically'. While sharing information is crucial for creating value, it pays to be cautious, starting with low-cost information, and only sharing further information if the other party is reciprocating. Making multiple offers is a particularly strategic manoeuvre for learning about the other party's interest and preferences. By offering the other party several packages of equal value to you, and asking which they prefer, it is possible to elicit information about the other party's preferences and priorities, while revealing little about your own (Lax and Sebenius 2006: 208). As noted above, however cooperative a negotiation, it is vital that negotiators do not divulge their walk-away point. Once the other party knows this, they have no incentive to offer anything more.

---

**Overcoming the negotiator's dilemma**

**Ask, listen and learn:** Find out as much about the other party and their preferences as possible.

**Divulge information strategically:** Be cautious and only share information if the other side reciprocates; offer multiple packages of equivalent value to yourself in order to elicit information while giving away little.

**Offset your defensive demands against their defensive demands:** Offer to make a concession in a sensitive area only if they make a concession in one of theirs.

---

A third piece of advice is particularly relevant to trade negotiations, and aims to help developing countries defend themselves against being pressured into making concessions in sensitive areas. It emerges from Mexico's experience of negotiating NAFTA, in which it fought (successfully) to exclude the energy sector from liberalisation, a sector that the United States wanted to see liberalised. The first tactic Mexico used was to offset its defensive demands against the United States's defensive demands, rather than against its own offensive claims. Thus, rather than 'giving up' some of its offensive claims in order to exclude its energy sector from liberalisation, Mexico argued that its decision to exclude energy from liberalisation matched the US decision to exclude maritime transportation. In effect, Mexico argued that it was only prepared to liberalise its energy sector if the United States liberalised maritime transportation, a sector that Mexico knew was extremely sensitive to the United States (Ortiz Mena 2006).

The second tactic Mexico used was to bring a new issue into the negotiations in which it knew that the United States would not make concessions. Before the negotiations began, Mexico intimated that it wanted to bring migration onto the agenda. As expected, the United States steadfastly refused, and this gave the Mexican negotiators a clear basis from which to argue that it too could exclude energy liberalisation without making any concessions. Negotiators advise countries to always include some peripheral issues in the negotiating agenda that are of little value, but which can be used to camouflage true interests, or which can be put forward as a concession (Ortiz Mena 2006).

A wider question that trade negotiators have to weigh up is how much energy to invest in trying to create value as opposed to claiming as much of the value as possible. Given the vulnerabilities associated with sharing information, it might appear reasonable for developing countries to focus exclusively on value-claiming tactics. However, studies of asymmetric negotiations suggest that smaller parties often do better if they pursue a mixed strategy (seeking to both create and claim value) rather than a strategy that relies exclusively on trying to claim value (Odell 2006: 17).

There are two principal reasons why a mixed strategy is likely to be more effective. First, focusing exclusively on claiming value leads to a negotiation focused on brinkmanship and pressure tactics, which smaller countries are more likely to lose. To succeed in such a high-stakes negotiation, a country must have reliable intelligence on the walk-away point of the other party. It also requires that the smaller country is prepared to respond effectively to the pressure tactics from other parties that its hardball approach is likely to provoke. Second, and in contrast, a mixed strategy creates some value for the other party, providing it with some gains to take home and give to their domestic constituents, making agreement more politically feasible (Bhuglah 2004). The risks of relying exclusively on value-claiming tactics are illustrated in recent WTO negotiations (Case Study 18).

### Case Study 18: The challenges of claiming value: developing country coalitions at the WTO

The Like-Minded Group (LMG) was a coalition of between 8 and 14 developing countries that was particularly active between 1998 and 2000, in the run-up to the launch of the Doha Round of WTO negotiations. Some of the coalition's demands were offensive, calling for immediate redress of imbalances, development concerns and systemic reform of the WTO, while others were defensive, resisting the introduction of the 'Singapore Issues' and labour rights and opposing the launch of a new Round before their concerns were addressed.

The LMG adopted a strategy that relied exclusively on value-claiming tactics, including opening with a very ambitious set of demands in many areas; arguing that developed countries should make concessions out of concerns for legitimacy and justice rather than mutual gain; and holding the priority issues of the European Union (EU) and US hostage by threatening to block consensus if their demands were not met. Demands were presented as a take-it-or-leave-it package, and there was no discussion in the group of fall-back and concessions.

In response, the United States and EU could have rejected the demands outright, but this would have resulted in impasse which they considered costly. In order to avoid completely conceding, an option they also considered costly, they offered to compromise in some areas, and used a variety of tactics to try and split the LMG coalition. The LMG opted not to compromise and eventually fragmented, unable to stand the pressure. Although the LMG was able to shift the terms of the debate in some areas, overall it obtained very few concessions and, crucially, it failed in its core aim of preventing the launch of a new Round before previous imbalances had been addressed. Had the coalition been able to maintain unity and agree to compromise in some areas towards the end, it may well have been more successful.

*Source*: Narlikar and Odell (2006).

## Continually anticipate and adapt

Effective negotiators anticipate and adapt to changes during negotiations. It is tempting for negotiators to transpose a strategy that proved to be successful in one context to a subsequent negotiation, but this can be a costly mistake. For each negotiation, experts emphasise the need to make a fresh diagnosis and tailor their strategy accordingly. Moreover, as negotiations take place in a continually evolving context, and the interests and objectives of other parties at the table can change during the negotiation, it is important to adopt a flexible approach (Odell 2000; Bhuglah 2004).

*For each negotiation, strategists emphasise the need to make a fresh diagnosis and tailor their strategy accordingly.*

Indeed, the most successful negotiators are open to signals and new information emanating from the negotiation, looking for changes in the external environment and working to propel negotiations in favourable directions (Devereaux et al. 2006b). Bearing this in mind, negotiators should plan regular breaks during the negotiations to re-group, reflect and adapt their strategy.

In general, small developing countries may be at a tactical advantage when it comes to selecting an appropriate negotiating strategy. Weaker parties in a negotiation are often more sensitive to relative power, and are usually more accurate in perceiving the behaviours and attitudes of their negotiating opponents than those with more power (Zartman and Rubin 2000; Thompson 2012).

Negotiators can glean valuable information whilst inside the negotiating room, by carefully monitoring the other party to discern shifts in their negotiating strategy and underlying interests. Assessing the counterpart is a constant task for a negotiator, and requires actively listening and being attentive to the tone, body language and words utilised (Bhuglah 2004). While this may sound obvious, in many instances negotiators exhibit 'cognitive closure', where they downplay information that contradicts their prior beliefs, failing to notice shifts in the approach of the other parties.

Outside of the negotiating room, tracking political and economic developments in the partner country may also provide valuable insights into likely shifts in the counterparty's interests, BATNA and strategy. In the United States, for instance, tracking the positions of key legislators and interest groups helps reveal the degree of political support for a government's negotiating position. It is also possible to keep track of internal political timetables and use opinion polls to watch political trends that may affect the negotiating approach.

---

**Anticipating and adapting**

**Are the interests, priorities and strategy of the other party changing?** Is any shift discernible in the negotiating room? Are there any political and economic changes in their country that prompt a shift in their interests or strategy?

**Are there any political or economic changes at home or internationally that change my country's interests?**

**Is my relative power position weaker or stronger than before?**

**How are changes affecting my BATNA?** Should I cultivate other options? How should my negotiating strategy change in response?

---

In addition, negotiators need to track the way in which shifts in the political and economic context affect their own objectives and relative power position, including their BATNA. A major shift in the domestic political landscape may result in a negotiator being given very different instructions and objectives. For instance, when a new left-wing political party came to power in Bolivia in 2005, it led to dramatic policy change in trade. Bolivia opted to exit from preferential trade relations with the United States and EU (Gray Molina 2010).

Changes in international markets can significantly affect the relative power of countries at the table. Therefore, market conditions need to be continually monitored for changes that could open new opportunities and risks. For instance, during the Lomé negotiations between Europe and African, Caribbean and Pacific (ACP) countries in the early 1970s, a rapid rise in the world price for sugar dramatically improved the negotiating position of the ACP sugar exporters. Almost overnight, ACP countries went from being exporters of a commodity in chronic over-supply to being exporters of a foodstuff that was in short supply (Mahler 1981). ACP negotiators capitalised on this shift and derived significant benefits from the resulting Sugar Protocol.

Mexico's experience of negotiating a free trade agreement with the United States helps to illustrate the various ways in which political and economic shifts can significantly affect negotiations (Case Study 19).

---

**Case Study 19: The impact of economic and political shifts: Mexico's FTA negotiations with the United States**

In the early 1990s, Mexico negotiated an FTA with the United States (NAFTA). Mexico was the main *demandeur* in the negotiations and was prepared to make concessions in many areas. However, from the outset it was determined to keep its oil sector out of the negotiations, and it largely succeeded. One of the lessons emerging from the NAFTA negotiations on energy is the way in which changes in the external economic and political environment have the potential to affect the negotiating process.

Changing oil prices were the most pressing economic concern for Mexican negotiators. During the NAFTA negotiations, the United States was engaged in the Gulf War, and Mexican negotiators were acutely aware that protracted political instability in the Middle East would drive up world oil prices and lead the United States to increase the pressure on Mexico to open up the sector. In the event, the war ended successfully from the US perspective, and oil prices did not reach problematic levels.

Paradoxically, as Mexico's public finances were heavily reliant on oil revenues, low oil prices also posed a problem. The negotiators were aware that if the oil price fell significantly (which it did) then their government would be in a delicate fiscal position, and the United States would be able to press hard at the negotiating table, knowing that the Mexicans needed an agreement to calm the markets. In anticipation of such a problem, Mexico purchased oil futures ahead of the negotiations, which helped it to avert this scenario.

In terms of politics, the US elections, scheduled for late 1992, loomed large over the NAFTA negotiations. As the initial *demandeur* of an agreement, Mexico was eager to complete negotiations and see the agreement ratified under the incumbent Bush administration, fearing that a change in government would impede an agreement. In a bid to secure agreement well before the elections, the Mexican negotiators made a series of concessions early in 1992, arguably caving in too early, although they still held out over energy. The United States, recognising this weakness in the Mexican strategy, opted to play for time rather than conclude an agreement.

As the US election grew closer, the tables turned. President Bush became desperate for an agreement as economic recession had eroded his popularity and he was keen to present a NAFTA agreement as a political success. By August 1992, the United States was in haste to conclude an agreement, and this helped Mexico to avoid commitments in energy, even at the very end of the negotiations.

*Source*: Ortiz Mena (2006).

## (Re)frame the negotiations in your favour

Ideas are a potent source of power in a trade negotiation, yet this is often overlooked (Tussie and Saguier 2011). Shaping the way that negotiations are framed, in other words the mental windows through which we view reality or a particular problem, is a particularly powerful way of influencing outcomes. Frames are developed on the basis of arguments, analogies and metaphors, all of which define both the problem to be solved and the range of possible solutions. By tapping into preconceived beliefs and attitudes, framing works by elevating the importance of some and suppressing others (Harvard Business Essentials 2005).

Successful framing or re-framing of issues during a negotiation changes the way that the parties and other relevant groups perceive them. For instance, during the TRIPs negotiations, developing countries successfully shifted the debate from one about piracy and the theft of ideas, to one about health and access to lifesaving medicines (Odell and Sell 2006). Re-framing the negotiations in this way helped developing countries to secure concessions, including on the right of governments to export medicines produced under compulsory licenses to countries that lack production capacity. While it is possible for the framing of an issue to directly influence the perceptions of negotiators, it often works most effectively when it operates via public opinion and so it is worth accompanying such moves in line with an effective media strategy.

---

**Framing**

**Can our interests be framed in terms of fairness?** Fair outcomes (reciprocity versus proportionality) or fair process (all states have the right to participate)?

**Are there popular issues or international commitments that we can link to?** Development, public health, access to education, food security?

**Can we use the values espoused by trading partners** to our advantage?

**Do we have a framing strategy?** For example, press releases, regular press briefings, op-eds, forging alliances with NGOs and cultivating a group of friendly journalists and public opinion leaders?

---

Framing issues in terms of widely held values such as 'fairness' or other types of objective criteria is particularly powerful (Fisher and Ury 1991). Appealing to concepts of 'fairness' or 'justice' is especially likely to elicit support from the broader public when there are obvious vast asymmetries in power or levels of development between the negotiating parties. The power in framing a proposal as 'fair' is that it sounds objective and legitimate, yet there are many competing conceptions of fairness and they can be selected in order to pursue subjective interests. For this reason it is important to identify the conception that is best suited to one's interests and whenever the other party invokes a particular notion of fairness, provide an immediate counter-argument so that their frame is not adopted as the legitimate one.

In the trade context, developed countries have long argued that the norm of reciprocity is fair because it ensures that all countries undertake the same level of commitment. Developing countries have countered this by pointing out that reciprocity is only fair when the parties are equal, proposing a new norm of proportionality on the grounds that it is a fairer way of determining commitments when the parties are fundamentally unequal (Narlikar 2006).

Another powerful technique is to frame an issue by relying on the arguments put forward by large countries in other contexts and requesting that they 'practice what they preach'. When campaigning for changes to the TRIPS Agreement, for instance, campaigners sought to have ministers reaffirm public health commitments that they had made in other fora and that could be undermined by provisions in the TRIPS Agreement. Meanwhile in the cotton case, the argument of the four cotton-exporting African countries was powerful because it was framed in terms of upholding the core values of the international trading system, including competitiveness and free trade (Case Study 20).

---

**Case Study 20: The power of framing: the African cotton initiative at the WTO**

Cotton subsidies became one of the key issues of the Doha Round of WTO negotiations, which was surprising, not least because it was championed by four least-developed countries (Benin, Burkina Faso, Mali and Chad) that had not previously played a significant role in WTO negotiations. Even though their efforts have, to date, been unsuccessful in securing changes in US cotton subsidies, the experience of these countries provides an excellent illustration how framing an issue effectively can help push it up the negotiating agenda.

The African cotton exporters had one ace card in their relations with other members: they were internationally competitive producers. After accounting for the effects of subsidies, African cotton is up to three times more competitive than that produced by the United States. The African countries used this to their advantage, pointing out that while they were among the most competitive producers in the world this competitiveness had been 'virtually nullified by the refusal of other cotton-producing countries to accept market forces and competition as defined in the WTO's objectives, by maintaining high levels of support for production and export'. They called for full liberalisation and denounced all forms of cotton border measures, domestic support and subsidies. These rallying calls were powerful because they reflected the values and principles that developed countries frequently refer to in the trade context.

The contrast between the so-called genuine competitiveness of the C4 and the 'artificial' competitiveness of the United States made for a very effective diagnostic frame, one that would repeatedly trouble US negotiators. As one adviser to the African countries noted, 'How could you be against this argument? The Africans only asked that the United States and the EU apply those global trade rules to themselves. I think that was a very powerful statement, especially coming from a group of least developed countries'.

*Source*: Eagleton-Pierce (2011).

## Make sound technical and legal arguments

Information and expertise can be important sources of power in a negotiation, and this is especially true for trade negotiations given the complexity of the terrain. They can be used to persuade other parties to change their position, and to defend a party from tactics that rely on misrepresentation.

When seeking to convince others to shift their opinion through rational persuasion, four factors are important. First, an argument needs to be seen as credible by the other party. Conveying a high level of information and expertise enhances credibility. This might include showing that ideas have been thoroughly researched, citing trusted sources, displaying mastery of the technical language, teaming up with credible allies and sharing personal experiences. Second, a detailed understanding of the target audience and their likely reactions is required. Third, arguments must be solid. They need to be logical and consistent with the available facts, favourably address the interests of those you seek to persuade and anticipate and refute likely objections. Finally, it helps if the person delivering the message has exceptional communication skills that captivate the other party (Harvard Business Essentials 2005).

Applying this to trade negotiations, it is helpful to consider whether there is evidence that the other party deems particularly credible that can be used to your advantage. For instance, when negotiating with the EU it can be particularly effective to cite studies by the World Bank or International Monetary Fund as the EU considers these institutions to be particularly authoritative. Although the position of these organisations is not always in line with those of developing countries, there are some areas where the arguments they advance are similar, including on rules of origin, the temporary migration of labour (Mode 4) and intellectual property rights. Capitalising on these arguments can provide leverage.

---

**Using information and expertise to influence**

**Is my argument credible?** Have the ideas have been thoroughly researched? What trusted sources can I cite? Are there credible allies I can team up with?

**How is my target audience likely to react?** How do my proposals fit with existing laws and practices of the other party?

**Is my argument solid?** Is it logical and consistent with available facts? Does it favourably address the interests of the other party? Have I anticipated and refuted likely objections?

**Are my proposals legally and technically sound?** Have they been scrutinised by top-quality lawyers? Economists?

**Do I have the requisite communication skills?** If not, can someone else present the argument?

---

Drawing attention to the economic and social disruption that could be caused in your country as the result of accepting the proposals of your counterparts can be an effective way of way of persuading other countries to back down. As one small state negotiator explained, 'If you can show others in your group that you have a visible, critical national issue and can explain your position, others will generally find a way out for you. In such a case, even when you are small and weak, something will be done to accommodate you' (Jones et al. 2010: 60).

To maximise the likelihood that a technical proposal is accepted, it is useful to think through how a given proposal will be received by technocrats on the other side. Having a detailed understanding of the relevant laws and decision-making procedures in the other country can be a valuable asset in a negotiation, and one that is often overlooked. This knowledge can be used to craft proposals that will fit the institutional requirements of the other party, making it more likely that technical-level officials will accept arguments (Odell 2000: 217–218).

Access to accurate information and attention to technical detail is also crucially important in evaluating the proposals and offers made by other parties, particularly at the drafting stage. In some instances, offers may appear generous but the value is eroded in practice by the 'small print'. For instance, industrialised countries have made much of their provision of duty-free-quota-free access to imports from least developed countries. Although the schemes sound very generous, many studies show that for most countries their actual benefits are negligible due to product exclusions and complex rules of origin. It is therefore critically important to keep a very close watch on the selection of words, twists of sentences, deliberate loopholes in punctuation and ambiguous expressions. To influence the final text, a negotiator should have several alternative formulations of a text prepared in advance, from which to make counter-proposals.

In drafting and responding to proposals, a core objective should be to preserve as much 'wriggle-room' for your party as possible, and to close down that of the other side. Particular care should be paid to questions of enforcement. A challenge for developing countries is to try and obtain commitments from developed countries that are enforceable. Often, developed countries agree only to language such as 'will endeavour to' or 'may' (known as 'best endeavour clauses'), which are non-binding and hence unenforceable. Alternatively, commitments may be binding but terms used may be vague, or there may be no effective mechanism for monitoring, weakening potential for enforcement. For instance, while the WTO TRIPS Agreement contains binding commitments on technology transfer, lack of clarity over the definition of key terms and an absence of effective monitoring has meant that the provision has had very limited impact (Case Study 21).

*In drafting and responding to proposals, a core objective should be to preserve as much 'wriggle-room' for your party as possible, and to close down that of the other side.*

In general, the experiences of small developing countries underscore the importance of having skilled lawyers on the team. For instance, when Mexico negotiated NAFTA, it had extremely capable economists but an area of vulnerability was a lack of understanding of the complexity and nature of the US legal system. As a result, Mexico lost some significant gains that had been made at the negotiating table when the negotiated text was turned into domestic legislation in the United States. It is crucial to have top quality legal advice about the counterparty's laws and this is at least as important as sound economic advice. 'While it is likely that any well-trained economist will understand the impact of negotiation commitments on his or her home country, a small mistake by lawyers regarding long and complex texts can have dire consequences' (Ortiz Mena 2006).

**Case Study 21: Challenges of legal drafting and enforcement: TRIPS provisions on technology transfer**

Technology and innovation play an increasingly important role in the global economy, yet least developed countries (LDCs) face a growing technology gap, which hinders their development. This challenge is recognised in the WTO TRIPS Agreement, which gives LDCs special consideration, both in the Preamble and Article 66.2. The latter stipulates that 'Developed country Members shall provide incentives to enterprises and institutions in their territories for the purpose of promoting and encouraging technology transfer to least-developed country Members in order to enable them to create a sound and viable technological base' (TRIPS Article 66.2).

Even though Article 66.2 creates a binding legal obligation on developed countries to support technology transfer, the drafting of the article leaves developed countries with a high level of 'wriggle room', and, together with a lack of clarity and consensus over the definition of the key terms used, and the absence of an effective monitoring mechanism, this means that little has been achieved.

Under this article, developed country member governments are not obligated to carry out technology transfer themselves, but rather are to provide incentives to their 'enterprises and institutions' to encourage technology flows to LDC members. This leaves room for legal disagreement on the extent to which countries are responsible for the impact of the incentives they provide. In addition, it is not clear which countries are considered 'developed' and therefore obligated under the article. While the UN provides a clear, regularly updated list of countries classified as LDCs, the WTO does not formally classify countries as 'developed'.

There is also no clarity over the 'incentives' that should qualify as fulfilling Article 66.2. Nor is there a standard WTO or TRIPS definition of what comprises technology transfer, and efforts to reach international agreement on such definitions have long met with frustration. One of the key problems of the lack of definitional clarity is that any activity can be stretched to qualify as technology transfer. Moreover, even if there was agreement on these definitions, the text of Article 66.2 does not specify what level of activity would satisfy its requirements, and there is no clear and objective way to set that yardstick. How many incentives are enough? How much technology transfer should occur? Do best efforts suffice, or must technology flows pass a certain threshold? How should such variables be measured?

The weak implementation of the technology transfer provisions in the TRIPS Agreement, even in the presence of a binding obligation, highlight the importance of legal drafting and the strength of monitoring and enforcement mechanisms.

*Source*: Moon (2011).

## Use personal behaviours and attributes

The personal behaviours and attributes of a negotiator can exert significant influence over the behaviour of other parties in a negotiation. Negotiators need to be aware of both the ways they can use these qualities to influence others and how other parties are seeking to influence them. Tactics that rely on manipulating a person's self-identity can be effective as they often catch people off-guard. Studies suggest that while negotiators in positions of low power are more vigilant and better at collecting information and diagnosing negotiating situations than those in high-power positions, they are often more affected by the emotions of the other party. This can cause them to lose focus and yield ground when confronted by a stronger, emotional counterparty (Thompson 2012).

A reputation for trust and credibility is a valuable negotiating asset. Trade negotiators emphasise that professional circles are small, negotiations are rarely one-off and you are likely to meet the same people time and again. For this reason, it is crucial to think about the reputation you are establishing. In particular, the more a negotiator is seen as being credible, the more likely it is that their counterparts will listen to them. While this entails being candid, meaning what you say, and ensuring you are not perceived by other parties as misrepresenting facts, it is also important to retain sensitive information (Bhuglah 2004: 19).

Maintaining credibility as a negotiating team is also crucial, and for this, a united position must be maintained in public at all times. A team's credibility is damaged by an aura of disunity, disagreement or other forms of dissension. Any sign of difference within a team provides an opportunity that the other party is likely to exploit.

During interviews, negotiators from developing countries dwelt on the importance of bringing a tenacious attitude to the negotiating table: be bold and take initiatives, be pushy where necessary, sustain commitment to negotiations and not get discouraged. One negotiator described an effective negotiator as follows:

> ... they have very strong political characters that are able to ask what needs to be asked. They don't just sit back. They are not complacent. They will ask, they will enquire and they will push.
>
> (Jones et al. 2010: 23)

While some negotiating texts advise negotiators that they should not show anger, others argue that displays of anger can be effective. Used at the right time, anger can be a very effective way of concentrating the minds of those around the table on the seriousness or urgency of the situation.[1] The key is to ensure that any anger is used tactically, as part of a carefully thought out strategy, rather than the result of personal animosity. In a situation where a negotiator is concerned that personal animosity is likely to fuel their desire to escalate conflict, it is often wise to let others take the lead (Malhotra and Bazerman 2007).

---

**Personal behaviours and attributes**

**How are my current actions and behaviours affecting my reputation?** How can I improve my reputation for credibility and trust?

**What is my team's reputation?** Are we maintaining a unified position in public? If not, what steps can we take to address this?

**Am I being tenacious?** Am I using active listening skills to solicit information from others? Have I taken steps to build rapport with the other party?

**Is there a risk I, or others in my team, are being co-opted?** Am I being flattered? Am I maintaining sufficient professional distance from the other party?

---

To elicit information from the other party, negotiating texts emphasise the need for actively listening to others, rather than merely focusing on communicating your position to them. Strategic use of silence can be used to great effect. Many people find silence uncomfortable and will attempt to fill it, often providing useful information as they do so (Fisher and Ury 1991: 117–118). In addition, asking open-ended questions can help solicit information from the other party.

Some tactics work at a personal level and leverage the fact that people have an inherent need to be liked, approved of and respected. While such factors may seem trivial at first, a series of psychological studies suggest that we should not underestimate the fact that negotiators are more likely to make concessions to people that they know and like, and to people who look like and behave like them. For this reason, many texts advise negotiators to dress in a similar manner, and match the body language and verbal style of the other party. People are also more likely to respond favourably when flattered (Thompson 2012: 154–157). However, negotiators caution that care is needed in using such tactics as they can appear patronising and backfire.

Getting to know the other party on a personal level through social events can affect behaviour in the negotiating room, as it helps people to develop trust. Negotiators give many examples of progress being facilitated by the lead negotiators developing trust and understanding during social occasions.

Just as negotiators should look to use such tactics, they should be aware that they can also be targets. Negotiators should continually be on the lookout for the use of subtle tactics by others, and guard against the possibility that they shift their behaviour in response. For instance, they should be wary of sharing personal information during social gatherings lest it be turned against them in the negotiating room. Similarly, while building rapport with the other party helps facilitate communication, it is important that negotiators are not co-opted by the other party.

Individuals can reduce the risks of co-option by maintaining 'professional distance'. One practical way of doing this is for negotiators to identify someone that they trust, and who is not involved in the negotiation, has no stake in its outcome, and request that they act as a devil's advocate, critically appraising their negotiating strategy (Malhotra and Bazerman 2007). Governments can minimise the risks of their negotiators being co-opted by ensuring that they are not isolated from the rest of government in their day-to-day activities, that there is a strong system of oversight and that they are held accountable for their negotiating outcomes. This is particularly important for small developing countries given that most have very few staff in overseas missions, communication with capital is often irregular and oversight poor (Jones et al. 2010).

*While building rapport with the other party helps facilitate communication, it is important that negotiators are not co-opted by the other party.*

Finally, negotiators from the smaller party need to guard against becoming hostage to a mindset of powerlessness or helplessness. When facing a party that has far more resources, it is common for negotiators to feel overwhelmed and pessimistic about their chances of influencing outcomes, and they underperform as a result. In some cases, negotiators may not be aware of the assumptions they are making about their relative power position, but they can nonetheless have a negative impact on performance. Not only will they demand less, but they are also more vulnerable to influencing tactics and threats. In the words of one expert, 'those who "think weak" inevitably also "act weak"' (Malhotra and Bazerman 2007: 255).

## Negotiating across cultures

Culture is the unique character of a social group – the values and norms shared by its members and which set it apart from other groups. It profoundly influences how people think, communicate and behave. Although we usually associate cultures with countries, other social groups often have their own distinct sub-culture, including industries, professions, families, organisations and regions.

Recent research highlights a risk that negotiators give *too much* weight to broad nationality-based stereotypes about culture (Program on Negotiation at Harvard Law School 2009). For instance, some books tell negotiators to expect Germans to be reserved, hard-bargainers who may be offended by personal questions and tardiness, and Mexicans to use an expressive communication style and a lengthy rapport-building.

Relying on such national stereotypes gives rise to several problems. First, while these stereotypes often contain a grain of truth, they are highly unlikely to apply to trade negotiators who, by definition, have broad international experience. Second, by focusing on national stereotypes, negotiators may overlook more pertinent information (see box). A counterpart's profession or aspects of their personality, for instance, often turn out to be a better indication of their negotiating style than their nationality. Third, even if cultural factors play a role, it is often the differences in legal traditions, political systems, the interests of community groups and business norms that matter, rather than stereotypes about personality traits (Lax and Sebenius 2006; Program on Negotiation at Harvard Law School 2009).

**Possible cultural differences that can impact negotiations**

**Direct versus Indirect Communication.** Are messages communicated explicitly and directly or in a nuanced and indirect manner that relies, for instance, on analogy or metaphor? Will they ask direct questions or rely on gleaning information from our reaction to proposals? Is the other party likely to say 'no' directly or remain silent to indicate dissent?

**Formal versus Informal Style.** Is using first name terms appropriate? How formally does the other party usually dress for this type of negotiation?

**Egalitarianism versus Hierarchy.** Does the leader of the other party make the decisions, or are they made through team consensus? How much deference is given to political status? How many levels of approval does the outcome of the negotiation require?

**Contract versus Relationship.** How much importance does the other party place on building social relationships both inside and outside of the negotiating room?

Rather ironically, in some situations, negotiators try 'too hard' to overcome perceived cultural differences. The literature contains some amusing anecdotes of all the parties around a table simultaneously making attempts to accommodate differences, finding themselves at cross-purposes as a result (such as a meeting between NGOs and government officials where the former dress in formal suits and the latter dress casually).

A challenge for developing country negotiators is to work out the prevailing culture and sub-cultures in each forum where they expect to negotiate, and tailor their style accordingly. In the international investment sector, for instance, an investor might bring a dispute against a state in the WTO dispute settlement mechanism, or in the World Bank's arbitration arm the International Centre for Settlement of Investment Disputes (ICSID), or in a private arbitration institution, such as the International Chamber of Commerce (ICC). There are vast differences in organisational cultures, partly as a result of the professional background of officials: while those adjudicating in the WTO usually have backgrounds in public policy, those in the ICC are typically drawn from the private business sector. Thus an argument that might be well received and considered valid organisation in one might not be valid in another.[2]

In preparing for a cross-cultural negotiation, it may be helpful to identify the areas in which there salient differences that may affect the negotiation. In particular, it is often helpful to anticipate differences in strategy and tactics that may cause misunderstandings, and think about how to avoid them or deal with them if they do arise.

## Pressure tactics

There are many tactics and tricks that are used in a negotiation to try and take advantage of the other party, which can be referred to as 'pressure tactics'. Experienced negotiators emphasise the 'harsh reality' of negotiating trade agreements with much larger states (Case Study 22). New negotiators should not be under any illusions; they need to be aware of the various types of pressure tactics that they are likely to come under, and to think through ways to respond. Forewarned is forearmed.

Pressure tactics can be divided into five broad types (see box). Coercive pressures are the first and most obvious. They include threats by other countries to withdraw aid, trade preferences or other forms of material support; or threats by foreign investors to relocate or to take a government to international arbitration. In some cases, the other party may go over the heads of the negotiators, and make threats directly to senior political figures. In such situations, there is the risk that a minister or head of state will be convinced to make valuable concessions because they are not technically conversant with the issues (Bhuglah 2004: 32).

---

**Five types of pressure tactics**

**Coercive threats:** Threats to withdraw unilateral trade preferences, aid, concessionary finance; threats by companies to relocate.

**Ultimatums:** Presenting a template text on a take-it-or-leave-it basis. Insisting on the inclusion of clauses at the last minute so there is too little time to analyse them.

**Deliberate deception of facts or intentions:** Provision of biased or misguiding information or evidence. Flooding other party with vast amounts of information in order to confuse.

> **Biasing the negotiating set-up:** Negotiating through the night to exhaust smaller delegations. Excluding the most technically competent from the negotiating room.
>
> **Personal attacks:** Asking someone to continually repeat himself or herself. Interrupting negotiations to do something else. Questioning a negotiator's competence.

The second involves ultimatums. Very often a party will threaten to walk away from a negotiation or to withhold their consent unless a concession is made. Threatening to leave is a tactic that can work for the smaller party, although it must be used with care. In particular, it is important that the other party genuinely believes that the small country is willing to walk out, and for this it is crucial that the small state has a substantial BATNA (or at least the impression of one) to give the threat credibility.

Other ultimatums involve the presentation of a template text on a 'take-it-or-leave-it' basis, or insisting that a series of clauses be added at the very last minute, without giving the other party time to make a detailed assessment before they have to respond.

A third set of tactics centres on the deliberate deception of facts or intentions: presenting evidence in a misguiding or false manner, or suggesting that one will act in certain manner when there is no intention to do so. A common version of this tactic is to deliberately mislead other parties as to the degree of delegated authority a negotiator has: negotiators allow their opponents to believe that they have full authority to make concessions. Then, only after they have pressed their opponents as hard as they can and worked out what their opponents believe to be a firm deal, do they let their opponents know that they have to get authorisation from someone else (Bhuglah 2004: 32).

In trade negotiations with larger states, negotiators note that information and advice provided under the guise of technical assistance may be biased towards the interests of donor countries (Jones et al. 2010). In other instances, parties may attempt to flood their negotiating opponents with information, much of which is irrelevant, in a bid to overwhelm and distract them. Alternatively, they may leak information to the media in order to confuse their negotiating partner. As they face significant asymmetries in access to information and expertise, small developing countries may be particularly targeted by such tactics, particularly if large states assume that resource constraints will prevent them from cross checking information and advice.

A fourth set of tactics revolves around hard-line tactics to influence the negotiating set-up. For instance, a negotiating partner may try to find ways to exclude the most technically competent people of the other party from the negotiating room. Indeed, in some negotiations, large states have insisted that only ministers are allowed to take the floor, knowing full well that their ministers are far better briefed in the details than those of the other party.

The final set of tactics involves making personal attacks. This includes attacking the status of the other party by making them wait for you or by interrupting the negotiations to deal with other people; implying that the other party is ignorant or inexperienced; calling their professional qualifications into question; or refusing to listen and making the other party repeat themselves (Fisher and Ury 1991).

*How should negotiators respond to such tactics?* Studies show that people who are unaccustomed to dealing with such tactics are likely to respond in one of two ways. First, and most common, they tolerate the threat, giving the other side the benefit of the doubt, or getting angry and acquiescing this time but promising oneself never to interact with the party again. A second common reaction is to respond in kind, so the situation escalates until one side capitulates or the talks break down. Neither response is optimal (Fisher and Ury 1991).

---

**Responding to pressure tactics**

*Coercive threats*

- Research thoroughly;
- Call the bluff of the other party if threats are not credible;
- Expose their actions to the public;
- Talk to their superiors.

*Ultimatums*

- Know your options and alternatives, and those of the other party;
- Do not act in haste, fully explore all options;
- If the threat is credible, make a cool-headed and objective decision on whether to exit, based on your objectives and alternatives.

*Deception*

- Assume information and advice is biased unless there is reason to believe otherwise;
- Cross-check and verify with own information or from trustworthy third parties;
- Share experiences of deception with other small countries – forewarned is forearmed.

*Biased set-up*

- Ask the other party to justify the negotiating structure/rationale and prepare to counter-argue;
- Propose alternative options;
- Insist discussions on negotiating set-up are transparent;
- Make the biases public.

*Personal attacks*

- Acknowledge them.

More effective responses involve neutralising or diffusing pressure tactics. Negotiators can often take steps to address coercive threats and ultimatums. First, it is important to establish whether they are credible. In cases where a threat is deemed not to be credible and where the government has a strong legal position, it may be possible to call the bluff of the other party, as Costa Rica did with a US oil company (see Case Study 5). When threats are credible, it may be possible to neutralise them by exposing them to public scrutiny, including by leaking them to the media. In some instances, ministers or heads of state have diffused a threat by talking directly to their counterparts to request that a negotiator issuing threats inside the negotiating room be brought into line.

Whenever an attempt is made to get another party to back down from a threat, it is important to think through a face-saving strategy for that party. In the absence of a way to avoid embarrassment of humiliation, the other party is likely to be very reluctant to change position. To maximise the likelihood that the other party changes position, it is helpful to provide the other party with a legitimate, face-saving way to frame their decision to change course (Malhotra and Bazerman 2007).

In responding to information-based tactics, vigilance is key. The starting point for defending oneself against deception is to assume that information and expertise from the other party is biased unless there is good reason to think otherwise. As two negotiation professionals argue, 'unless you have reason to trust someone, don't' (Fisher and Ury 1991). Negotiators should cross check and verify information from the other party (including leaks, as these too might be deliberate). For this, it is crucial that they have access to their own sources of information, or can access reliable information and advice from a trusted third party. Small developing countries may also benefit from logging and sharing instances of factual misrepresentation for future reference.

*The starting point for defending oneself against deception is to assume that information and expertise from the other party is biased unless there is good reason to think otherwise.*

### Case Study 22: The harsh reality of negotiations: personal reflections

During discussions, experienced negotiators noted the importance of communicating the 'harsh reality' to those new to the world of trade negotiations. One negotiator kindly offered to share two of his experiences from negotiating Economic Partnership Agreements (EPAs) with the EU:

*The Pacific capitulates to the EU's pressure tactics*

'In late October and November 2007 the EU moved to assure completion of interim Economic Partnership Agreements with great urgency as the WTO derogation would expire on 1st January 2008. Peter Mandelson, the European Trade Commissioner and an extremely tough negotiator, fulfilled the EU mandate to complete the negotiations. During the Pacific negotiations he forced the Pacific Trade ministers to remove their main technical experts from their negotiating room as they were seen as a threat to an expeditious end of the negotiations. The Pacific ministers capitulated to every one of his demands including some of the most onerous restrictions on developmental measures such as the use of export taxes and infant industry issues.'

*Being 'stabbed in the back'*

'The Pacific ACP countries nominally had a unified negotiating mandate. However during the Economic Partnership Agreement negotiations, Papua New Guinea and Fiji broke away and negotiated behind the backs of the rest of the region. This move was driven by representatives of the private sector from Papua New Guinea, who were always part of their negotiating team, and who spoke on behalf of the Papua New Guinea government. Their representative, who knew nothing about trade law, basically negotiated behind the back of the other Pacific officials, to secure an agreement with the EU that protected market access for fish products and sugar from Papua New Guinea and Fiji. While the other ACP countries received no benefits, Papua New Guinea received the global sourcing rule for tuna products and for this, they were willing to sign virtually any agreement.'

*Source*: Personal reflections of Roman Grynberg, Senior Research Fellow, Botswana Institute for Development Policy Analysis, and former Director of Economic Governance, Pacific Forum Islands Secretariat.

## Anticipate the future

When negotiating the details of the text, it is important to think about the entire lifetime of the agreement. As the external environment does not stop evolving once an agreement is reached, the agreement needs to be created in a way that enables it to respond and adapt to evolving circumstances (Lax and Sebenius 2006: 149).

A responsive agreement can be created by including clauses that provide for commitments to be automatically suspended, or reviewed and modified, in response to external shocks or to changing preferences. In addition, exceptions clauses can help ensure that the treaty commitments will not prevent a government from pursuing important policy objectives. Clauses can also set out the grounds on which a country can reasonably exit from the agreement or a date at which the agreement will expire.

While the inclusion of such clauses is standard in trade agreements, their scope varies, and the challenge for developing country negotiators is to anticipate their country's needs in advance and tailor provisions accordingly. For instance, they may wish to ensure that the provisions refer to specific shocks to which their country is prone, such as low monetary reserves, natural disasters, a decline in tariff revenue or sudden capital flight. Or they may wish to ensure that there are specific exceptions for important policy objectives such as fostering infant industries, ensuring food security or addressing social inequalities.

---

**Crafting a responsive agreement**

- Are there clauses that enable my country to **unilaterally suspend commitments in order to address external shocks** (e.g. low monetary reserves, natural disaster, financial crisis, food insecurity)?
- Are the **exceptions sufficiently broad to cover priority policy objectives?**
- **Are there clear provisions for modifying the agreement in future?** Where does the power for such changes reside?
- **How readily can my country exit from the agreement?** Are there procedures and conditions for exit?

---

In thinking about the future, consideration should also be given to shaping the institutional set-up that will govern the implementation of the agreement. The complexity of the arrangements varies across agreements. For instance, the Economic Partnership Agreement between the EU and fifteen Caribbean countries specifies a relatively elaborate framework, including a Joint Council (ministerial level), Trade and Development Committee (senior officials), Parliamentary Committee (members of parliament) and a Consultative Committee (academic, economic and social actors). In designing the institutional set-up, negotiators need to consider how much decision-making authority to give to the various actors, and the ways in which their responsibilities are specified. A common concern raised by developing countries, for example, is that trade agreements often adopt a narrow approach to monitoring and evaluating implementation, mandating institutions to measure this against the parties' respective commitments, rather than against the agreement's wider objectives (such as its contribution to sustainable development).

Recent developments in investment treaties underscore the importance of designing responsive agreements. In the 1980s and 1990s, many developing countries signed bilateral investment treaties that guaranteed foreign investors an unfettered right to transfer their capital. During the recent financial crises, concerns have been raised that such clauses may constrain the ability of countries to respond, including through the use of capital controls (Ostry et al. 2011). Without provisions in the treaties outlining how clauses could be renegotiated or modified, states were left with a tough choice: abide by the treaty, renege on their obligations or attempt to exit. Exit was not an appealing option for many governments as they feared that announcing the termination of an investment treaty would send out powerful negative signals to foreign investors – something that policy-makers facing a financial crisis are keen to avoid. Moreover, even they did choose to try and exit, most investment treaties have survival clauses, which mean the treaty is still in force for another ten or twenty years on all investments made prior to the termination.

For bilateral investment treaties and free trade agreements that contain investor-state clauses, it is particularly important to think proactively at the drafting stage about how the provisions of a text might be interpreted by an arbitration panel in a future dispute. This is an matter of increasing consequence as increasing numbers of international arbitration cases are being lodged against developing country governments.

---

**Shaping the outcome of future disputes**

- **How might an arbitration panel interpret key clauses** if this goes to dispute? How can we influence interpretation in our favour?

- Are there **joint instruments** that we should pursue that will reflect our policy priorities and concerns, particularly if they are insufficiently incorporated in the core text (e.g. side agreement, exchange of letters)?

- Are there **unilateral** measures that we can take (e.g. letters and memos to parliament, official statements)?

---

Under international law, states are the drafters and masters of their treaties. Thus, even in investment treaties where states have delegated the task of ruling on investor claims to arbitral tribunals, they retain a certain degree of interpretive authority: they can clarify their authentic intentions and issue authoritative statements on the proper reading of their treaties. Considering these issues at the drafting stage can be crucial for influencing the outcome of future disputes, and negotiators can shape interpretation by providing a clear roadmap for future interpreters both in terms of substance and procedure (Alschner 2011).

The most obvious way to influence future interpretation is to use farsighted and precise treaty language and to specify clear interpretation guidelines. For instance, countries may opt to make specific reference in the text to agreements in other fields of international law such as environment or human rights, thereby ensuring that obligations arising under these treaties are also considered at the point of interpretation.

However, even if such language is not used in the treaty text other instruments can be used. Joint acts and statements by the contracting parties are considered to be reflective of their intentions and, as such, they must be treated as authoritative in international disputes. Formal instruments such as side agreements that create direct legal obligations between the contracting states have the greatest legal weight. The Canada–Panama FTA, for example, is supplemented by two side agreements on labour and the environment, which must be considered during arbitration. Informal instruments that are agreed upon at the conclusion of the treaty, such as an exchange of letters or verbal notes, can also inform interpretation.

While a country cannot unilaterally give authoritative meaning to treaty terms, in the absence of conclusive joint interpretations, some unilateral documents or statements may be used to guide treaty interpretation, particularly if they are made during the course of the ratification process. Letters and memos to government or legislature, commentaries, official statements and parliamentary debate may shed light on the meaning of provisions (Alschner 2011).

## Stay vigilant

A final lesson for negotiators to think about 'at the negotiating table' is to be vigilant in the way they manage key information during the negotiation, and in following the negotiations through until the very end.

---

**Stay vigilant**

Have we taken **steps to protect the confidentiality** of key documents?

Are we using **secure methods of communication**?

Are our **politicians briefed** on the key technical details?

Have significant changes been made during **'legal scrubbing'**?

---

The previous sections have emphasised the need to keep sensitive information, including negotiating mandates, details about alternatives and negotiating strategy, confidential. Yet, in many cases developing countries inadvertently negotiate in the open. They rely on email and telephone conversations to liaise with colleagues, forms of communication which, senior negotiators emphasise, can be readily intercepted by their negotiating partners. One negotiator recounted an instance where a group of developing countries accepted the offer from their negotiating partner to use their offices for their preparatory meetings, discounting the risk that the negotiating partner may opt to listen in.[3] As this example suggests, it pays to think through the degree of access that your negotiating partners may have, and to adapt your communication methods accordingly.

During a negotiation, even the best negotiators can be caught off-guard by an unexpected question. In such moments, vigilance is key. Rather than respond under pressure, experts advise that it is best to say as little as possible until you find an opportunity to think more carefully about a response. For instance, one may simply respond, 'That's an interesting question. I'll have to think about the answer and get back to you' (Malhotra and Bazerman 2007).

Vigilance is also needed in the final stages of a negotiation, when there are several ways in which precious gains made at the negotiating table can be lost. In some instances, negotiators have won important concessions during the technical phase of the negotiations, only to see them lost when the negotiations come to the political stage, and politicians take the lead in concluding the final text, agreeing to apparently minor changes in the text without realising their significance.

Alternatively, concessions can be lost during the process of legal scrubbing. Although this is purportedly a neutral process designed to ensure that the text is legally consistent, it is sometimes used to make substantive changes to the text. For instance, there are reports that significant changes were made to the US–CAFTA and the US–Morocco FTA texts during legal scrubbing.[4] Gains can also be lost at the point at which the agreement is translated into domestic legislation. Such losses can be avoided by negotiators taking steps to carefully monitor the text of the agreement throughout the last stages of the process, including during implementation.

## Summary

This chapter has examined the moves a negotiator can make 'at the negotiating table'. It has shown that there is a wide range of tactics that negotiators can draw upon, and the suitability of each tactic depends on the specifics of the negotiation. Three lessons in particular stand out. The first is the importance of psychology; to maximise their leverage, negotiators from small developing countries need to be optimistic, creative, tenacious and to persevere. The second is the need to be thorough and vigilant, particularly with regard to scrutinising information and the moves of the other party. The third is the need to be responsive and adaptive, modifying your strategy and tactics in response to the moves of the other and changes in the environment outside of the negotiating room, and crafting an agreement that will stand the test of time.

So far, we have examined the steps to be taken before and during a given negotiation. The next chapter turns to address the longer-term challenge of strengthening government institutions, so that the country has the foundations in place for successful trade negotiations.

---

**Checklist: Moves at the Negotiating Table**

**Are we negotiating from rigid positions or our underlying interests?**

**Have we cooperated with the other party to identify areas for creating value?** Have we used a range of tactics to maximise value creation?

**How can we claim value in this negotiation?** How can we defend ourselves against value-claiming tactics by the other party?

**How can we frame this negotiation or specific issues to our advantage?**

**Are our proposals technically and legally sound?** Are there technical and legal flaws in the proposals of the other side?

**Are we leveraging our personal attributes and behaviours to the fullest extent?** Have we guarded against the risk of being co-opted by the other party?

**Have we considered how the culture of the other party might affect their negotiating strategy?**

**What 'dirty tactics' are the other party most likely to use?** What will our response be?

# 5
# Putting the Right Foundations in Place

To maximise their influence over the outcome of trade negotiations, it is crucial that developing countries put the right foundations in place. As experienced negotiators point out, it is extremely difficult to execute an astute negotiating strategy if political leaders are not sufficiently engaged, there are few skilled personnel in the trade ministry, information is of dubious quality or government institutions function poorly.

This chapter examines the steps that developing countries can take to tackle the underlying constraints that impede effective negotiation, even with relatively few resources. While negotiators have control over some of the reform measures proposed in this chapter, others rely on decisions being made by ministers. However, negotiators can be important advocates for reform, and it is hoped that some of the lessons from other countries will provide inspiration.

## Make the links between trade negotiations and development

As we have seen 'knowing your interests' is a vital pre-requisite for effective negotiation, yet negotiators from developing countries often find themselves working in the dark, with little clarity on their country's interests (Jones et al. 2010: 36).

This lack of clarity is often symptomatic of two deeper problems. First, policies in trade and related areas (such as industrial and innovation policy) are often poorly articulated. If there is no clear policy direction, and if it is not clear where and how international trade fits into the country's development strategy, then positions in trade negotiations are likely to be merely reactions to either the immediate needs of domestic lobbyists or the agendas set by other countries.

Moreover, if links between trade and the wider development policy are not clearly articulated, then there is a risk that trade will be seen as an end in itself. For instance, a country might negotiate successfully for increased market access for its services exporters, but if no attention has been paid to upgrading the competitiveness of these companies, they may not be able to make use of the new market access. As negotiators emphasise, it is vital that a country's negotiating objectives are clearly rooted in its wider development strategy; without this, any concessions gained in the negotiating room may turn out to have little value in practice.

*A country's negotiating objectives need to be clearly rooted in its wider development strategy; without this, any concessions gained in the negotiating room may turn out to have little value in practice.*

Setting out a clear policy direction for international trade, and making this a publicly available statement that is regularly updated, provides an important reference point for negotiators and stakeholders alike. Forging such a policy requires strong political leadership. While it is vital to solicit inputs from stakeholders, they typically have narrow and relatively short-term interests. Ideally, government should take a broader view, filtering competing interests, identifying short-term priorities and working with key stakeholders to determine the long-term policy direction (Mkandawire 2010). Developing a medium-term vision and strategy for the role international trade should play in a country's wider development is a challenging process, yet Mauritius has managed this process effectively for many years (Case Study 23).

---

**Ensuring sufficient priority is given to negotiations**

**Are there clear national priorities for trade negotiations?** Is there a **section on trade in the national development strategy**? If not, how might this be developed?

Are there clear **policies in areas related to trade (e.g. industry, agriculture, innovation)**? If so, how might these policy objectives be furthered during the negotiations?

Are politicians fully informed about the **salience of the trade negotiating issues for national development**? What steps can be taken to increase awareness among politicians and the wider public?

A second problem is that political leaders do not always give the appropriate level of priority to trade negotiations, given their country's economic situation and its aspirations. For instance, trade negotiations should arguably be made a relatively high priority for countries with a development strategy that focuses on expanding value-added exports. In contrast, trade negotiations might be less important (at least in the short-term) for countries that depend overwhelmingly on the export of natural resources.

Political leadership is crucial as it galvanises the government machinery into action. When the executive and other senior figures in government are convinced of the importance of trade issues, it is more likely that the trade ministry will be given an influential minister, trade issues will be considered in foreign policy decisions, the performance of trade officials will be monitored more closely and greater human and financial resources will be allocated to trade (Bhuglah 2004; Dunlop et al. 2004; Bilal et al. 2007; Jones et al. 2010).

*What steps might negotiators take to ensure these two problems are addressed?* One very concrete step that negotiators can take to is to highlight the links between the issues on the negotiating table and their country's wider development objectives. Particularly in the poorest and most resource-constrained countries, the intricacies of trade negotiations can seem a world away from obvious and urgent challenges such as tackling food security and creating jobs. The highly specialised and technocratic language of trade negotiations exacerbates this gap. Negotiators can help ensure that political leaders and the wider public are aware of the relevance of trade negotiations by setting out, for instance, how proposals on intellectual property rules might affect access to new technologies by local manufacturing firms, or how agricultural export subsidies impact the competitiveness of local farmers.

Negotiators may also be able to advocate for clearer policy direction for trade negotiations, by encouraging their ministry to actively participate in the formulation of national development strategies and policies. For instance, Ghana's Ministry of Trade and Industry has championed the creation of trade and industry policies that the ministry and related government department and agencies pursue, and these provide clear policy direction to trade negotiators. The ministry led the formulation of these policies and then secured high-level buy-in, ensuring that the policies received cabinet approval.[1]

**Case Study 23: Managing integration with the global economy: lessons from Mauritius**

Mauritius faced severe constraints when it obtained independence in 1968, including a low level of economic development, commodity dependence, and isolation from key international markets. Challenges were so severe that James Meade, a Nobel Prize-winning economist, declared the country's prospects to be dismal. Yet Mauritius defied these pessimistic predictions. Since the 1970s, it has sustained average annual growth rates of 5 per cent, average per capita incomes have tripled, poverty rates have fallen dramatically and inequality has reduced markedly. The economic structure has been transformed, from agriculture to manufacturing and high-end services.

How did this happen? Mauritius is small and highly dependent on external trade. Like other African countries, Mauritius benefitted from significant preferences into the European and US markets for key exports, but Mauritius stands out for manoeuvring to maximise the benefits it derived from these preferences. In the 1970s, government and the sugar industries successfully negotiated with European countries to obtain the highest sugar quotas of all African, Caribbean and Pacific (ACP) countries, gaining rents that were equivalent to as much as 13 per cent of its GDP in some years.

Crucially, profits from the sugar sector were used to stimulate the development of manufacturing. In 1970, an export processing zone (EPZ) was created, which took advantage of textiles preferences provided under the Multi-Fibre Agreement, and had an unusually high level of investment from local entrepreneurs. Interestingly, the government adopted a two-pronged strategy, and, in parallel to a range of initiatives to promote exports, it protected the domestic economy. As the manufacturing sector took off, employment opportunities increased dramatically, particularly for women, and together with a strong trade union movement that pushed for wage increases and a strong social security system, this contributed to reductions in poverty and inequality. By the 1990s, manufacturing had become the main driver of the economy.

Since the 1990s, in anticipation of the erosion of preferences for sugar and textiles, Mauritius sought to diversify further, and the government initiated a range of policies to promote the development of offshore banking and financial services, high-end tourism and business process outsourcing. It has also liberalised trade and, in doing so, it has used a range of policy instruments, including fiscal, monetary and education, to facilitate the adjustment process and respond to economic shocks.

Two features of the Mauritian experience stand out. First, government and local industrialists appear to have worked hand-in-hand in pursuit of long-term change. Second, it is striking that the government constantly searched for new drivers of growth and ways to harness changes in the global economy to its advantage. As one analyst argues, 'Mauritius's impressive economic performance has not been an accident, but rather the result of careful planning and policies' (Zafar 2012).

*Sources*: Rodrik (2001), Subramanian (2009) and Zafar (2012).

## Improve cross-government coordination and accountability

Effective cross-government coordination and strong accountability can help developing countries channel their limited resources to best effect during trade negotiations The experience of Pakistan in the late 1990s illustrates the costs that can arise from weak cross-government coordination (Case Study 24).

### Case Study 24: The costs of poorly coordinated institutions: the Pakistan–US textile dispute

In 1998, the United States imposed quantitative restrictions on imports of combed cotton yarn from Pakistan under the (now-expired) Agreement on Textiles and Clothing. Pakistan immediately took action to challenge the quotas: first through bilateral negotiations with the United States, then through the non-binding dispute settlement mechanism under the Agreement and, finally, through the WTO dispute settlement mechanism.

When the dispute began in 1998, Pakistan had no office solely responsible for WTO affairs or trade-related disputes, either at the Ministry of Commerce or at the permanent mission in Geneva. It lacked officials with sufficient legal or diplomatic experience of international trade and the WTO to coordinate the dispute case or undertake legal research, and it had no institutional framework to coordinate between the Ambassadors in Geneva and Washington, the Ministry of Commerce and the Pakistani textile industry.

Recognising these problems, the government hired an external consultant who had both the background and expertise to manage the case and the personal connections to effectively coordinate between all the parties involved. The Pakistani government and textile industry also felt it was necessary to hire teams of Washington- and Geneva-based international lawyers to provide legal advice. However, due to the ad hoc way in which the Pakistani case was organised, there was no predetermined process to decide how to hire and pay for further outside expertise. Locating, negotiating with and finding funding for outside legal counsel created delays and extra costs.

Although Pakistan eventually won the case, poor institutional coordination had contributed to a series of delays in pursuing the case, with the result that the United States was able to impose the (illegal) quotas for two years and nine months (almost the maximum of three years provided for under the Agreement). Pakistan clearly had a strong case and, had its institutions been stronger and better coordinated, it is plausible that the quotas would have been lifted earlier.

*Source*: Hussain (2005).

Measures to improve coordination and accountability can be taken at several levels. Clearly assigning responsibility for international trade negotiations to a specific ministry and setting out the functions that need to be fulfilled can substantially improve coordination. Ideally, this would be accompanied with the appointment of a strong and competent minister, and adequate financial and human resources. Turf battles may take place if there is not clarity over responsibilities or a clear lead ministry. During the cotton negotiations, for instance, Benin's negotiating team was frustrated by a lack of effective coordination between the Ministry of Trade, which led on WTO negotiations in the capital, and the Ministry of Foreign Affairs, whose ambassador led negotiations in Geneva (Jones et al. 2010: 31).

Countries follow different approaches in allocating responsibility for international trade negotiations, each with advantages and disadvantages. In some countries, responsibility is assigned to the Ministry of Foreign Affairs and this has the advantage of ensuring clear links are made between trade and wider foreign policy objectives. This arrangement also makes it less likely that the minister and officials are side-tracked by domestic political concerns, since foreign trade is separated from domestic trade issues such as rising import prices. The disadvantage is that officials may not have much day-to-day interaction with domestic stakeholders, making them less aware of the interests and needs of firms and other stakeholders.

---

**Key functions of the ministry responsible for international trade negotiations**

- Taking the lead in trade negotiations on behalf of government;
- Horizon scanning and tracking international trade to determine which trade negotiations are upcoming, relevant and important;
- Collecting and analysing information;
- Formulating international trade policies;
- Soliciting input from across government and from stakeholders outside government;
- Disseminating information on trade negotiations across government and to stakeholders;
- Drafting negotiating mandates and proposing them to the executive;
- Formulating negotiating positions and ensuring they are technically and legally sound.

---

Another common approach is to assign responsibility for trade negotiations to a ministry of trade and industry. This has the advantage of creating a strong link between trade and industrial policy, but it poses the risk that the ministry will be focused on resolving the challenges faced by domestic producers, and place less emphasis on international affairs. Finally, in some cases, trade negotiations are assigned to the Office of the President. This provides negotiators with high-level political buy-in, but runs the risk that negotiations will occur in isolation from the ministries responsible for foreign affairs and wider trade and industrial policies.[2]

Improving coordination among negotiators based overseas, the network of missions in third countries and technical experts based in the capital is similarly vital for negotiating effectively (Panke 2011: 300–301). Ideally, negotiators based overseas send regular and substantive reports back to capital on the pertinent issues on the negotiating table and the positions of other parties, and make detailed and specific requests for input and guidance; and capital-based officials, in turn, provide prompt and sufficiently detailed feedback to their overseas negotiators. This improves the quality or negotiating positions and helps ensure the accountability of trade representatives. It reduces the risk that over time, trade officials located in overseas missions become isolated from their home country. Isolation increases susceptibility to coercion or capture by larger states or lobby groups.

---

**Improving cross-government coordination and accountability**

**Clear roles and responsibilities for international trade:** Is responsibility for leading trade negotiations clearly assigned to a single ministry? Are the functions that this ministry needs to fulfil clearly set out?

**Capital mission:** How regular is communication between capital and mission? Are negotiators and capital-based officials adequately informed about and effectively feeding into each other's work? Are relevant missions in third countries brought into the network?

**Cross-government:** How effective is the mechanism for consulting other government institutions over trade negotiations? How much input does it provide to negotiators? Can it be made more efficient? How can negotiators be provided with real-time input from key government institutions?

**Parliament:** How regularly are parliamentarians briefed and consulted on trade negotiations (particularly those on relevant trade or foreign affairs committees)?

In periods of intense negotiation, discussions and feedback may be needed several times a day, including outside of office hours. In practice, the level of communication varies starkly across countries. Some negotiators report that missions and capitals 'communicate every day, often more than five times' and during intense periods of negotiation this includes regular and direct contact with the minister or prime minister, even out of hours. Other negotiators face a very different reality. Severe delays in responses from the capital undermine the formulation of negotiating positions and negotiators are left to use their own discretion, with minimal guidance or instructions. As one Brussels-based negotiator lamented, 'I don't think we ever got comments [from capital] in time.' Another Geneva-based negotiator noted that, in the absence of directions from the capital, 'my interventions are based on my experience, not my government's position' (Jones et al. 2010: 29–30).

Some developing countries ensure that the expertise of capital-based officials is available during negotiations by including them on the negotiating team. However, the cost of sending a large team abroad is prohibitive for many countries. In these cases, effective use of information and communication technology can help ensure that a country's full expertise is available for the small team of negotiators at the negotiating table. For example, one small island state makes its top experts, including lawyers, available to the negotiators remotely. The negotiators inform the experts when the negotiating session will take place, and they make sure they are available and at their desk. Negotiators then send questions from within the negotiating room to the experts based back in capital by Blackberry (which is a more secure system for messaging than many other mobile phone platforms) and they receive real-time responses.[3]

Negotiators also note that commercial attachés based in third countries are often overlooked as a source of information and support. Commercial attachés can provide valuable insights and contributions, particularly when the country they are based in is playing a key role in a negotiation. Greater efforts could be made to ensure their expertise and intelligence is utilised.

The ever-increasing scope of trade negotiations makes cross-government coordination more valuable than ever. Trade negotiations are becoming relevant to the work of a whole range of government institutions. For example, negotiations over intellectual property are directly relevant to the work of health ministries (access to generic drugs); agriculture ministries (access to seeds and other inputs, and protection of biodiversity); science, technology and industry ministries (access to technology, local research and development); education ministries (access to educational materials); intellectual property offices (charged with filing patents); and Attorney General's departments (charged with drafting legislation). In complex negotiations, determining the country's interests and hence its negotiating objectives demands an effective coordination mechanism that facilitates communication between the lead ministry and other relevant government institutions (Bhuglah 2004: 48).

Research suggests that while most small developing countries have cross-government coordination mechanisms, their efficacy varies greatly. While many donor initiatives have supported governments to establish formal mechanisms for cross-government coordination, they do not always function effectively (Jones et al. 2010: 30–31).

Part of the coordination problem is size. One concern is that so many parties are involved in the discussion, that it becomes unwieldy and inefficient. Rather than attempting to debate details of negotiations in large inter-agency committees, it may be more effective to create small working groups that can deliver timely decisions specific to the negotiating agenda. However, a proliferation of committees equally runs the risk of duplication. For this reason, one study suggests adapting existing cross-government coordinating mechanisms to include trade negotiations in their mandate (Bilal et al. 2007).

Although cross-government coordination often takes the form of a standing or ad hoc committee, communication can be facilitated by the use of electronic media. For instance, a government might set up a government-wide trade bulletin or newsletter, or a website where government stakeholders can keep up-to-date on trade issues and the progress of negotiations. Alternatively, confidential chat forums could be used to provide real-time communication between negotiators on mission overseas and government institutions in capital.

While emphasis is often placed on the creation of formal structures, negotiators highlight the vital role that strong informal professional networks can play. For instance, if a negotiator faces a tough question on agriculture and wishes to have immediate input from the experts at the Ministry of Agriculture, utilising a professional network of contacts can often provide a far more rapid response than relying solely on formal communication channels. This said, in relying on such informal networks, negotiators should ensure that they are available and used by the whole negotiating team; if a network is built around an individual negotiator there is the risk that its value will be lost when that individual leaves.

Parliaments are the final element of effective coordination and accountability. Parliaments play an important function of keeping the executive in check, and in many small developing countries their consent is required for an international trade agreement to come into effect. However, parliaments are often neglected during consultation over trade policies and research suggests that the quality of parliamentary oversight is variable (Jones et al. 2010: 33).

If parliamentarians are well informed and able to adequately scrutinise trade agreements, the wider public is more likely to perceive the outcome of trade negotiations as legitimate. Indeed, ensuring that parliamentarians are on board from the outset should be an integral part of each negotiating strategy: Good relations with parliamentarians can assist negotiators in preventing a favourable agreement from being derailed at the ratification stage. Conversely, the involvement of parliament can help negotiators credibly use the prospect of non-ratification when the deal on the table is unfavourable.

## Recruit and retain high-calibre trade officials

It is hard to overstate the importance of having a high-calibre negotiating team, and establishing such a team is one of the most important steps that a country can take to improve its influence over negotiations.

Many small developing countries have relatively few officials working on trade, which poses challenges. A survey of representatives from more than 30 small developing countries suggests that on average these countries only have four officials working on trade negotiations in their capital, and the majority have two or fewer officials working on trade in their missions in Geneva. Indeed, 20 small developing countries are members or observers of the WTO yet they do not have a permanent presence in Geneva (Jones et al. 2010: 20–25).

A high level of turnover among trade negotiators often compounds personnel shortages. Turnover is high either because officials are rotated to other positions within the civil service or because they exit from the civil service to join other organisations (Jones et al. 2010: 20–25). This is a particular concern given that negotiating experience is one of the most important attributes of an effective negotiator. Retention problems are often symptomatic of wider problems within the civil service. In some small developing countries poor career prospects, low pay and low morale contribute to the exit of high-calibre officials (Mkandawire 2010). The importance of recruiting and retaining skilled negotiators is illustrated in the contrasting experiences of Mauritius and Ghana (Case Study 25).

Although full-scale civil service reform is clearly far beyond the mandate of trade negotiators and their ministers, several steps can be taken within ministries responsible for trade negotiations to address human resource constraints.

Given that experience and technical expertise are such highly valued attributes in a trade negotiator, it is important to ensure that negotiators remain in place for significant periods of time and, given the highly technical nature of many trade negotiations, are able to specialise. Interviews highlight a concern among some negotiators that they are moved around too much within the civil service and are unable to build up the necessary expertise to excel in trade negotiations, which is a source of frustration and demotivation. One concrete and relatively simple measure might be to create a cadre of specialised trade negotiators, who only move around within the trade negotiating team.

In instances where trade negotiations are assigned to ministries of trade and industry, a position on the negotiating team is often highly sought after by junior civil servants as negotiators have the opportunity to travel frequently and attend high-level international meetings. In such cases, it may be possible to set higher entry requirements for positions within this team, facilitating the recruitment of high-calibre officials.

Improving rewards and prospects for career advancement may help to stem the exit of experienced negotiators. A common complaint of public officials in developing countries, including in trade ministries, is that good performance is not rewarded, which undermines their incentive to work hard and to stay in the civil service. In the absence of wider public sector reforms, it may not be possible to address remuneration levels but the trade ministry may be able to find other ways to increase the level of recognition given to hardworking officials and to facilitate the acquisition of specialised knowledge. During discussions, negotiators explained that relatively simple steps such as ensuring regular feedback from superiors, that work is assigned in accordance with skill sets, assisting officials to upgrade their skills through training, and giving negotiators public recognition when they have performed well, may help to boost morale and retention.

Inevitably, more experienced negotiators will leave or be reassigned at some point, and succession planning is needed to ensure this does not result in a serious gap. Negotiators emphasise the importance of senior negotiators allowing their junior colleagues to accompany them into the negotiating room so that they have exposure to the cut and thrust of negotiations from an early stage in their career. In addition, measures should be taken to develop institutional memory, keeping records from negotiations and documenting the lessons learned.[4]

---

**Recruiting and retaining high-calibre officials**

**Is staff recruitment or retention a problem?** If so, what practical steps can be taken to improve it? Is it possible to keep trade negotiators in post for longer periods? Is it possible to provide incentives?

**Are we adequately represented in major negotiating hubs?** Could we improve representation and cut costs by pooling resources with other countries?

**How can we use external consultants to best effect?** How can we improve oversight and management to ensure their advice is independent (unbiased), excellent quality and delivered in a timely manner?

**Are roles and responsibilities clearly assigned within the team?**

**In which countries should we place our staff?** Which are our most important trading partners? With which countries do we want to expand our trade relations?

**What steps are we taking to continually upgrade the skills of team members?**

---

Although a wide range of programmes provide training to negotiators, a common criticism is that they tend to focus on the technical details, and do not address the wider questions of which trade rules and provisions might be appropriate for countries at different levels of development, or the types of trade rules needed by countries that are particularly small and vulnerable. In addition, many training programmes have been criticised for being biased towards the interests of industrialised states (Tandon 2004; Deere 2005).

This suggests a strong case for developing countries advocating the establishment of training courses, provided by independent third parties, which would discuss international trade rules in light of the latest research on different aspects of economic development. For instance, in investment, the International Institute of Sustainable Development runs a well-regarded training in a different region of the world each year, which examines investment negotiations from a development perspective.[5] Consideration should also be given to south–south exchanges. If, for instance, another developing country has recently negotiated a specific issue area of interest and has built up considerable expertise, a temporary secondment might be an invaluable way of acquiring technical knowledge.

Once a core group of highly competent officials is established, the membership of the negotiating team can be supplemented by bringing in specialised technical knowledge from relevant private sector actors and independent experts. A survey of negotiators from small developing countries suggests it is common practice for developing countries to hire consultants. Nearly all the countries surveyed used donor-funded consultants, while more than three-quarters employed their own consultants (Jones et al. 2010: 25).

Negotiators caution that active management and oversight is crucial when working with external consultants. In the context of donor projects, it is still common practice for donor organisations to second their own staff or for donors to select the consultants they send to work as advisers in ministries in developing countries. This poses the risk that the work will be ill-suited to the needs of the developing country negotiators, that it may be biased, or that it might enable the donor country to have access to negotiating information that should be kept confidential. To minimise these problems, ministries could negotiate with donors to ensure that they are able to independently recruit, employ and pay experts (Page 2006, 2011).

Former negotiators and trade officials can also be an important source of expertise, although this is often overlooked. Many experienced trade negotiators leave the civil service to join regional organisations and international organisations such as the WTO Secretariat, the World Bank and UNCTAD (United Nations Conference on Trade and Development). Tapping into this network can provide valuable insights and advice.

*Former negotiators and trade officials can also be an important source of expertise, although this is often overlooked.*

For some small developing countries, the high costs of maintaining overseas missions results in serious personnel shortages (or indeed the total absence of personnel) in key negotiating hubs such as Geneva. Pooling resources can help increase overseas presence. Small developing countries can share office facilities to reduce overhead costs, or they can be represented collectively through the missions of regional organisations (Bhuglah 2004). The Pacific Islands Forum Secretariat and the Organisation of Eastern Caribbean States, for instance, both have offices in Geneva that represent the interests of their members. Although representatives of regional organisations do not have WTO recognition and cannot represent the region formally in negotiations (unless they represent a customs union), the region can designate one country to speak on its behalf, as the EU did long before it was a member.

---

**Case Study 25: The importance of retaining skilled negotiators: Mauritius and Ghana**

*Mauritius*

One of the reasons for Mauritius' strong performance in international trade negotiations is the quality of its core negotiating team. In recent years, the team has comprised approximately ten highly experienced negotiators, drawn from both public and private sectors. While governments and ministers have changed, the core negotiating team has remained highly stable.

Concentrating the responsibility for negotiations in a small, stable and tightly bound group creates an informal network of accountability among negotiators, enhances trust and concentrates trade negotiation experience. Core team members are highly esteemed negotiators and command great respect in diplomatic circles, providing further leverage. As one negotiator explained 'You can get the respect of others in Geneva, and this enables you to do more informally.' A potential risk is that so much institutional memory has been embodied in so few individuals over time that the trade policy process is vulnerable to disruption should those individuals leave their posts.

*Ghana*

By contrast, interviews with Ghana's negotiators reveal that, during the past decade, the core international trade team consisted of only five people and suffered from high staff turnover and frequent reshuffling. With regard to postings in Brussels and Geneva, one negotiator lamented that 'by the time that you get on top of the issues, your posting is ended'.

Negotiators felt that the high turnover made it extremely difficult for the team to acquire specialist, technical knowledge, particularly on complex new areas of negotiations, such as trade in services. There was also concern that negotiators often worked in isolation, and did not pass on their knowledge and skills.

These contrasting experiences underscore the importance of developing a tight-knit and stable negotiating team, with a strong *esprit de cours* and clear succession planning, so that new negotiators rapidly acquire the knowledge and skills.

*Source*: Jones et al. (2010).

## Strengthen the evidence base

A striking lesson that emerges from previous chapters of this guide is that developing countries need reliable access to a raft of relevant, up-to-date and unbiased information and policy analysis, both about their own country and those they are negotiating with. As one senior negotiator noted, 'Without excellent technical briefs, negotiation becomes an abstract exercise.'[6]

A range of information is needed, including detailed information on the negotiator's own economy and its potential, from the macro to firm level; on trends in the international markets and international trade negotiations; on international and domestic law and regulations; and intelligence on the interests and objectives of negotiating partners, key third countries and other trade negotiations.

Despite the vital importance of information, many developing country negotiators have limited access to information of the requisite quality. While most small developing countries produce significant amounts of data on trade flows, economic impact assessments, legal advice and diplomatic intelligence, the quality is variable. In a survey and interviews, many negotiators from developing countries said that the information generated by their own governments tended to be unreliable and that they depended on information from elsewhere. Trade flow data was most likely to be perceived as being good quality, while economic impact studies and legal advice were particularly likely to be regarded as being poor quality (Jones et al. 2010: 26–28).

There are many international organisations, policy experts and academics producing detailed policy analysis on various aspects of trade negotiations, including their likely impact on development. However, many trade negotiators and academics from developing countries express concern that the policy debate is dominated by the interests of industrialised countries, not least because they fund and have greater say in the governance and research work of major international organisations.[7] Moreover, while the Organisation for Economic Cooperation and Development provides a platform for research and sharing knowledge among industrialised countries, there is no institution of comparable strength among developing countries. The South Centre, based in Geneva, is a valuable resource, but its financial and human resource base is far, far smaller.

National think tanks and other research institutions can play an important role in informing policy debates at a national level. That said, in many countries they are marginal to the trade policy process because they are severely under-resourced and relatively little research is being conducted that is directly relevant to trade policy (Jones et al. 2010).

The experience of Bangladesh illustrates the need for good information and monitoring (Case Study 26).

---

**Case Study 26: The costs of not staying abreast of trade issues: Bangladesh's seafood sector**

In 1997, the EU imposed a temporary ban on import of shrimp products from Bangladesh on the grounds that its exporters were not meeting health and safety standards, a move that cost Bangladesh US$14.7 million in lost export revenues. This experience illustrates the risks of government and producers not staying abreast of international trade issues and underestimating their potential impact.

By the late 1990s, seafood processing was the second largest export sector in Bangladesh, with frozen shrimp alone responsible for 7 per cent of total exports. The majority of these shrimp exports went to the EU. Despite the importance of shrimp to Bangladesh's export-oriented growth strategy, the industry lagged behind global standards in terms of sanitary facilities, technology adaptation and training procedures. Although the government had worked with several international agencies to improve seafood safety and quality control, Bangladeshi shrimp exporters still suffered from problems with both real and perceived product quality and safety.

In the late 1990s, EU began to send signals to the Bangladeshi government that they were falling short of important health and safety standards, while the United States detained almost 150 shipments of frozen shrimp from Bangladesh for inspection. Although the Bangladeshi government warned the Bangladesh Frozen Food Exporters Association about these safety issues, it is clear that the seriousness of the warnings or of the changes necessary to the industry was not fully understood at the producer level. It therefore came as a shock to many producers when, in July 1997, following an EU inspection of the country's seafood processing plants, inspectors decided that 'consuming fishery products processed in Bangladesh posed a significant risk to public health in EU member countries' and placed a temporary ban on imports of shrimp products from Bangladesh.

Following the ban, the Bangladeshi shrimp industry had to implement a number of drastic changes to its production model in order to comply with EU standards. It had to move shrimp processing from local villages to sanitary factory facilities, and this entailed a massive upgrading of facilities and training of staff. The cost of this upgrade was estimated at US$18–US$20 million.

If the Bangladeshi government and shrimp producers had taken more efforts to actively monitor the changing standards requirements of their major export partners, they would not have avoided the cost of upgrading facilities, but they might have avoided the high cost of a temporary export ban.

*Sources*: Rahman (2002) and Cato and Subasinge (2003).

*How can developing countries improve their evidence base?* A plethora of data and technical information can be readily and freely sourced online (see the box 'Online sources'). International databases provide access to product-level trade flow data (goods and services). In addition, the websites of international organisations provide details on the legal texts of existing trade agreements (WTO, FTAs, BITs), and regular updates on trade negotiations, while individual countries publish information on government websites.

---

**Strengthening the evidence base**

**Online sources:** Have I fully exhausted options for accessing information online? Can we upgrade our Internet connection to improve access and processing speeds?

**Overseas missions:** What information should I ask them to gather? What is the most crucial information for us to have on our negotiating partners? By when?

**Government data:** How reliable is government data on trade and related areas? How easy is it to access? How can data collection and management be improved? Where might funding and expertise be sought to upgrade systems?

**Research institutions:** Which international organisations are producing analysis in this area? How independent is their analysis? Which local organisations are producing/have the potential to produce high-quality data on national and regional trade issues? How might their work be strengthened?

---

Overseas missions and diplomatic and business contacts can be valuable sources of intelligence, including on the interests of other parties at the negotiating table. This can be supplemented by online searches that may reveal detailed information about the trade policies of other governments; the opinions of key stakeholders in their constituencies; and the careers and interests of individuals on the negotiating team of the other party. The United States, for instance, publishes the reports of its '301 Committee', which highlight the leading concerns that the United States has with the policies of its trade partners.

Other information is best sourced domestically. It is critically important that the government generates reliable statistical data, including on exports and imports, consumer prices, employment and revenue from trade and other taxes. The quality of this data is a major determinant of the reliability of impact studies. In many small developing countries, basic data on imports and exports is often available, but the quality is variable, and in the case of many African countries, cross-border trade is inadequately captured. Meanwhile, reliable data on production and employment is often lacking. Upgrading systems for collecting statistical data would greatly strengthen the quality of information and analysis available to negotiators. Consultation with private sector and civil society organisations can also be a valuable source of information, and

sed below (see the section 'Manage and Improve Input from
').

---

**Online sources of data, information and policy analysis on trade and development**

*Trade data and information*

- Trade Map: www.trademap.org (trade flow data; indicators on export performance, international demand, alternative markets and the role of competitors);
- Market Access Map: www.macmap.org (customs duties, bound tariffs, tariff quotas, anti-dumping duties, rules of origin);
- Investment Map: www.investmentmap.org (foreign direct investment (FDI) data at the sectoral level, combined with foreign affiliates, trade flows and tariffs information);
- Standards Map: www.standardsmap.org (online tool that enables analyses and comparisons of private/voluntary standards);
- World Integrated Trade Solution: http://wits.worldbank.org/wits (accesses and retrieves information on trade and tariffs, an analytical and simulation tool to estimate consequences of changes in tariffs);
- Bridges Weekly News Digest: http://ictsd.org/news/bridges weekly (weekly trade news from a sustainable development perspective);
- WTO Legal Texts: www.wto.org/english/docs_e/legal_e/legal_e. htm;
- WTO Trade Policy Reviews: www.wto.org/english/tratop_e/tpr_e/tpr_e.htm;
- EU Trade Information (European Commission): http://ec.europa.eu/trade;
- US Trade Information (Office of the United States Trade Representative): www.ustr.gov;
- China Trade Information (Ministry of Commerce of Republic of China) http://english.mofcom.gov.cn.

*Selected sources of policy analysis*

- Centre for Global Development: www.cgdev.org;
- Commonwealth Secretariat: www.thecommonwealth.org;

- Conference on Trade and Development (UNCTAD): http://unctad.org;
- Economic Commission for Africa (UNECA): http://new.uneca.org;
- Economic Commission for Latin America and the Caribbean (ECLAC): www.eclac.cl;
- European Centre for Development Policy Management (ECDPM): www.ecdpm.org;
- International Centre for Trade and Sustainable Development (ICTSD): http://ictsd.org;
- International Institute for Sustainable Development (IISD): www.iisd.org;
- International Lawyers and Economists Against Poverty (ILEAP): www.ileap-jeicp.org;
- Overseas Development Institute (ODI): www.odi.org;
- South Centre: www.southcentre.org;
- Third World Network: www.twnside.org.sg;
- Trade Law Centre (TRALAC): www.tralac.org;
- World Bank: www.worldbank.org;
- World Trade Institute Advisers: http://wtiadvisors.com.

In the area of policy analysis, there are a wide variety of international organisations that provide research on international trade and development (see the box 'Online sources'). The challenge for negotiators is to ascertain the independence and reliability of this analysis. More generally, there are strong arguments for increasing the level of political and financial support for organisations that provide a platform for south–south research and knowledge sharing. At the national level, negotiators could help bolster local research and improve its quality by establishing formal links with researchers and encouraging donors to provide long-term support to local institutions to research trade.

## Strengthening regional collaboration

For many developing countries, particularly the smallest, cooperating with neighbouring countries is an indispensible source of leverage in trade negotiations.

Cooperation can take many forms. A relatively low level of regional collaboration occurs when countries hold ad hoc informal meetings to share information, but they stop short of adopting a common approach to the negotiations. Although information sharing can be valuable, this approach does not provide leverage in negotiations. It is likely to be most valuable (and indeed most feasible) where there are no ongoing regional integration efforts, so countries are reluctant to collaborate formally. For instance, countries across Eastern Africa, which do not have a single, common regional organisation, meet regularly to share information about WTO negotiations.[8]

More substantive collaboration occurs when countries negotiate as a regional coalition, and this can provide substantial leverage. For instance, ministers and national officials might meet regularly to agree on a common negotiating mandate, and appoint a single minister to act as the lead negotiator or spokesperson. In such cases, trade experts from regional organisations (such as the Economic Commission for West African States (ECOWAS) or the Pacific Islands Forum Secretariat (PIFS)) are likely to be drawn upon for technical and strategic advice.

The highest level of collaboration occurs when countries delegate authority for negotiations to a regional organisation, with member states providing an oversight function. This was the approach taken by the Caribbean states during the Economic Partnership Agreement (EPA) negotiations with the EU; authority was delegated to the Caribbean Regional Negotiating Machinery, which reported to regional trade ministers.

---

**Regional collaboration for trade negotiations**

- **Meeting on an ad hoc basis** to share information;
- Negotiating as a **regional coalition**, adopting a single negotiating approach and agreeing on a common set of negotiating objectives;
- **Delegating authority** to a regional organisation.

---

Each type of collaboration has advantages and disadvantages. Negotiator concerns focus principally on the tension between pooling sovereignty to provide greater leverage in negotiations and the accountability and legitimacy challenges that this can pose.

In a regional coalition, national interests are directly represented at the negotiating table, and this has the advantage that negotiators are familiar with national policies, as well as local politics and economics. However, national representatives may not be as specialised as technical officials drawn from regional organisations. Moreover, as national representatives are usually based in the capital, coordination can be a challenge and it can be hard to negotiate as a cohesive team. Weak coordination leaves countries acutely vulnerable to divide and rule tactics by the other party. For instance, as one negotiator from a small developing country explained:

> ECOWAS is made up of 16 countries. We rarely meet among ourselves before coming to Brussels for negotiating sessions. When we get there, we accept things and then go back and realise that we shouldn't have.
>
> (Jones et al. 2010: 51)

Delegating authority to a regional organisation has the advantage of ensuring team cohesion and coordination, with the result that the region is more likely to have a unified position and be less susceptible to divide and rule tactics. Regional organisations can also act as a hub for technical expertise. The disadvantage of this model is that negotiators may be less conversant with national-level priorities and constraints; so for this approach to work, effective input and oversight from the national level is crucial. Moreover, if oversight from the national level is weak, there is the danger of the negotiators being (or being perceived as being) co-opted by the other party, which reduces their legitimacy. This is particularly a risk if regional organisations are dependent on donor funding for their survival, especially when donors sit on the other side of the negotiating table. The experience of the Caribbean during the EPA negotiations shows how these tensions can play out (Case Study 27).

There are practical steps that small developing countries can take to leverage the advantages and minimise the risks of delegating authority to regional organisations. First, it is essential that the regional organisation is, and is widely perceived to be, accountable to member states. Accountability is likely to be strongest if the regional organisation is financed primarily by member states, and any external funding is supplementary and not integral to its survival. Members may be able to adopt innovate funding mechanisms. The ECOWAS Secretariat, for instance, is partially financed through a 'community levy', a 0.5 per cent tax on imports originating from outside of the region that generates revenue for the financing of activities of ECOWAS institutions.

---

### Strengthening regional organisations

**Financing:** How can we ensure financial sustainability? What steps can we take to ensure the regional organisation is financed primarily by member states? How can we insulate donor funding from the risk of political interference?

**Oversight:** What mechanisms can we create to strengthen oversight and accountability of regional organisations to member states? Who do regional organisations report to? Is there sufficient technical competence among those they report to for this to be effective? If regional officials are going to lead negotiations, is there a clear mandate and mechanism for regular (e.g. weekly) reporting?

**Input from member states:** What is the level of input from member states into regional trade policy and negotiating positions? How can the quality of input be improved, particularly from poorer members?

**Coordination across member states:** Is there a clear mechanism for coordinating trade policy across member states? How can member states ensure a unified negotiating position?

---

*Accountability is likely to be strongest if the regional organisation is financed primarily by member states, and any external funding is supplementary and not integral to its survival.*

Where external funding is used, care should be taken to ensure that the donor does not have a stake in the outcome of the negotiation. Support can be channelled through independent third parties or long-term trust funds to insulate it from political interference.

Second, it is crucial to establish strong mechanisms for coordination between member states and oversight of the regional organisation. Technical experts need to be guided by clear policy direction from capitals. Moreover, individual states need to understand what is being negotiated in order to ensure that their interests are met and that they will be able to implement the terms of agreement. In cases where officials from regional organisations take the lead in negotiations, they need to be given a clear negotiating mandate. In the final stages of an agreement, it is not realistic for the regional organisation to consult with every government on every minor change (Dunlop et al. 2004). It is also important that adequate oversight is maintained and that regional negotiators report back regularly to trade ministers.

In the EU, for instance, the 'Trade Policy Committee' (formerly the '133 Committee') is comprised of representatives from member states and regularly meets to decide regional trade policy and to monitor the work of European trade negotiators (see the box 'Oversight of regional trade organisations'). At present, few regional organisations involving small developing countries have this level of oversight.

---

### Oversight of regional trade organisations: the European Union Trade Policy Committee

The Trade Policy Committee of the EU oversees the work of European trade negotiators, who are officials of the European Commission. The Committee is made up of representatives from each member state, and these officials are directly accountable to their domestic ministers. The Committee operates on a formal basis, and considers papers submitted by the European Commission and member states.

The Committee meets on a weekly basis to discuss the full range of trade policy issues affecting the European Community, from the strategic issues surrounding the launch of rounds of trade negotiations at the WTO, to specific difficulties with the export of individual products. It also considers the trade aspects of wider Community policies in order to ensure consistency. Additionally, the Committee holds special meetings to consider more complex issues as such as trade in services and textiles in greater depth.

In the case of specific trade negotiations, Committee members help draft the negotiating mandate and other directives that determine what negotiators can and cannot do during negotiations (these are then approved by ministers); monitor progress and redirect negotiators when they feel they are straying from their mandate; consider and propose changes to the mandate and negotiating directives; and scrutinise and provide input into drafts of the negotiating texts.

*Source*: UK Department for Business Innovation and Skills (www. bis.gov.uk).

---

**Case Study 27: Regional organisations in trade negotiations: lessons from the Caribbean EPA negotiations**

The EPA negotiations were held largely on a region-to-region basis, with six regional groups of ACP countries negotiating with the EU. In the Caribbean, the Caribbean Regional Negotiating Machinery (CRNM), a body that was affiliated but organisationally distinct from the Caribbean Community (CARICOM) Secretariat, led negotiations. The team was led by the head of the CRNM and comprised officials from the regional organisation, national governments and some independent experts. A committee of trade ministers provided oversight.

Interviews suggest that the Caribbean team was highly regarded for having a high level of technical expertise and competence in trade negotiations. However, there were concerns about the level of oversight and accountability. Some negotiators raised concerns in interviews that technical oversight from trade ministers was relatively weak, resulting in a lack of clear political direction. Others argued that accountability of the regional negotiating team to member states was weakened by limited inputs from many members and noted that the capacity of individual Caribbean states to provide input to the negotiating team varied widely.

Some countries, such as Barbados, were cited as exhibiting a relatively high level of preparation, while other countries had very little knowledge or awareness of the EPAs. The smaller and less developed countries in the Organisation of Eastern Caribbean States (OECS) were cited as those least able to provide inputs. One interviewee stated, for instance, 'Often countries don't even have data and positions to give the CRNM. The OECS Secretariat tries to support but doesn't have intimate knowledge of the countries.' Some interviewees were concerned that in the absence of clear positions from member states, the CRNM and the wider negotiating team had to rely on their own discretion in formulating positions, leaving them open to accusations that the negotiators' personal views unduly influenced negotiating positions and strategies. Others argued that the regional negotiators pursued their own agenda. In the words of one national representative, 'they felt they knew better and . . . pressured member states to undertake further commitments'.

Concerns of weak oversight and accountability were exacerbated by the fact that the EU and other external donors financed a significant portion of the budget of the CRNM. Reliance on contributions from external donors, particularly from the EU, inflamed perceptions of a lack of accountability to local stakeholders and member states. One former minister asked, 'Ultimately how much clout can you have when they [external donors] pay the CRNM?' Even more directly, some civil society critics contended that the CRNM is 'a tool of the European Commission'. Comments from one regional trade official reflected a recommendation heard in several interviews: 'In future, top negotiators must be paid directly by governments, not those they are negotiating with.'

In response to these concerns, the CRNM was brought under the auspices of the CARICOM Secretariat, with the new 'Office of Trade Negotiations' being a specialised division that reports to the CARICOM Secretary General. Effective negotiation on behalf of a region arguably requires a higher level of input – in the form of policy guidance, political oversight, and financial contributions – from member states than was present during the EPA negotiations.

*Source*: Jones et al. (2010: 51); discussions with trade negotiators, July 2011 and April 2012.

## Manage and improve input from stakeholders

Earlier chapters of this guide have emphasised the important roles that domestic stakeholders (such as local firms, farmers, trade unions and consumer groups) can play in trade negotiations. These include the provision of expertise, including, in some cases, being directly represented on negotiating teams; providing financial resources, such as paying for legal representation in trade disputes; increasing leverage during negotiations, including by influencing public opinion; and helping governments to decide on the country's medium-term trade strategy.

Discussions with trade negotiators highlight three challenges in their interactions with stakeholders. First, there are political challenges of balancing the interests of strong lobbying groups with the wider national interest and the need to ensure political legitimacy. In some cases, ad hoc lobbying by strong groups rather than the country's long-term development interests drives the positions that countries adopt in trade negotiations. This is vividly illustrated in Bangladesh's experience of negotiating on rules of origin changes for the apparel sector (Case Study 28).

While large companies are often the most powerful lobbyists, donors can be an influential group too. Rather strikingly, a survey of negotiators from small developing countries showed that respondents perceived international donors to have the second highest influence over national trade policy. This is a cause for concern, particularly in trade negotiations where officials from governments that are bilateral donors sit on the opposite side of the table. The management of donor relations is discussed further in the next chapter.

*Rather strikingly, a survey of negotiators from small developing countries showed that respondents perceived international donors to have the second highest influence over national trade policy.*

Second, even when governments are open to and genuinely interested in consultation with a wide variety of stakeholders, many stakeholders do not come forward or, if they do, they do not have the technical capacity to provide relevant inputs. Third, when they do receive disparate inputs from all these groups, governments face the challenge of weighing up competing positions in order to determine trade policy objectives and negotiating strategy that strikes a balance between short-term economic and political needs and long-term development interests and aspirations.

*What concrete steps can governments take to manage and improve contributions from stakeholders?* A valuable lesson from studies of developing countries that have grown rapidly is that coalitions and alliances were formed between the state and the private sector around long-term national interests rather than short-term industry-specific interests (Mkandawire 2010). In Mauritius, for instance, to help shift the country out of dependence on sugar, the government encouraged sugar plantation owners to invest the capital they had accumulated into other sectors of the Mauritian economy, first textiles, and later tourism and financial services. By working with local entrepreneurs and encouraging them to invest in new sectors, the Mauritian government created a basis for cooperation with the private sector that focused on the maximisation of national growth in the medium-term, rather than the short-term defence of a single industry (sugar) (see Case Study 23). This highlights the need for governments to foster a discussion with key stakeholders, including local entrepreneurs, on long-term interests and economic opportunities, and how government can foster them in its trade policies and negotiations.

A particular challenge that governments face is the management of relations with groups that stand to lose from an agreement. For instance, a government may decide that it is in the national interest to let an uncompetitive sector die and take a corresponding decision in trade negotiations. This requires a careful strategy for communicating this to the group concerned, and supporting the resulting adjustment process.[9]

---

**Managing and improving input from stakeholders**

**Work with stakeholders to develop medium-term trade and development policies**, in addition to consulting on their immediate trade objectives;

**Strengthen the participation from small and medium size businesses**, farmers' organisations, trade unions and others who are inadequately represented in consultations;

**Actively manage powerful lobby groups** to ensure their interests do not dominate.

---

Governments can help increase participation from groups whose interests may be affected by the outcome of trade negotiations but who are usually absent from consultations on trade. While this furthers democratic ideals, it is also of practical relevance for negotiators. Wide consultation builds popular support and brings legitimacy to the final outcome of a negotiation. Including a broad array of stakeholders in the decision-making process and responding to their concerns helps avoid a situation where stakeholders (including ordinary citizens) feel that the changes and reforms resulting from a trade agreement have been forced on them, reducing the likelihood of popular resistance (Dunlop et al. 2004: 10).

Working with, and strengthening, apex organisations, including private sector associations and trade unions, can be an effective way to raise awareness among broader constituencies of small firms, consumers, producers and workers (Dunlop et al. 2004: 10). In Barbados, for instance, the government has taken a series of measures to strengthen inputs from the private sector. It created a dedicated 'private sector trade team', which raises awareness of the key issues in negotiations among private sector organisations and channels inputs from the private sector to government. In addition, the government provides financial support to a series of business associations, including niche services industries that are central to the government's vision for future development (Jones et al. 2010: 40).

While negotiators are generally supportive of receiving higher levels of inputs from private sector organisations, particularly small- and medium-scale producers who are often poorly represented, many have an ambivalent response to the involvement of civil society organisations (predominately NGOs). Some consider their interventions to be unhelpful on the basis that civil society organisations do not understand the issues, are too radical in their demands or follow the agenda of western NGOs. A significant concern is the extent to which NGOs have legitimacy and genuinely represent sectors of society (this can also be a concern with private sector organisations). Where they were considered helpful, negotiators welcomed the information civil society groups provide, their ability to raise awareness and, in some cases, their ability to reinforce the government's negotiating position by mobilising popular support (Jones et al. 2010: 41).

### Case Study 28: The challenges of pursuing a 'national' interest: Bangladesh and the textiles industry

'Ready-Made-Garments' are a major export for Bangladesh. As a 'least developed' country, Bangladesh has received preferential access to the European market since its independence in 1971, and in the last decade, full duty-free quota-free access to the European market for all products except arms through the EU's 'Everything But Arms' scheme. However, until 2010, the EU's rules of origin required that, in order to qualify for preferential treatment, ready-made garments had to be made from fabric and yarns made either in Bangladesh or in the EU.

While this requirement benefited the Bangladeshi textile industry, it drew criticism for constraining the ability of garment exporters to fully utilise European trade preferences. Bangladeshi textile manufacturers were unable to produce the amount of fabric yarn necessary to meet the demand for exports of ready-made-garments. In addition, the price of these inputs was substantially higher in Bangladesh than neighbouring countries. As a result, it was sometimes cheaper for exporters to source fabric and yarn abroad than to utilise trade preferences. Although the Bangladeshi production mills invested to expand their capacity, preference utilisation rates remained relatively low.

Producers of ready-made garments continually lobbied government to advocate a relaxation of the rules of origin so that they could source cheaper inputs from elsewhere; however, such a move was inimical to the interests of the textile companies. While Bangladeshi economists recognised the importance of moving the economy towards higher-value added sectors, political leaders relied on the support of, and often had close personal ties to, textile manufacturers. As a result, the government was criticised for supporting the interests of the textile industry over the interests of the ready-made garments exporters.

In the early 2000s, the EU proposed relaxing rules of origin to allow sourcing of inputs from across the South Asian region, but the measure was opposed by the Bangladeshi government, despite the fact that studies had predicted that such a move would provide net gains due to the expansion of the garments sector that would result.

In 2010, the EU went ahead with changes that enable garments exporters to source inputs globally, a move which was welcomed by the garments sector but heavily criticised by the Bangladeshi textile industry.

This experience highlights the challenges for governments of balancing the interests of different elements of the domestic private sector, with short-term political considerations often coming before long-term economic priorities. This is a challenge that is familiar to many negotiators, from developing and industrialised countries.

*Sources*: Bhattacharya et al. (2004), Haider (2007), Harun (2010) and Haroon (2011).

### Use technical assistance to your advantage

The majority of developing countries draw on donor support during trade negotiations, and this takes different forms, including the use of consultants, studies and training programmes that they provide.

Negotiators emphasise that the use of donor assistance is a double-edged sword. On one hand, many argue that, in the face of severe financial and human resource constraints, such support is invaluable. As one negotiator notes, 'During the Uruguay Round, smaller delegations could not have achieved what they did without the provision of technical assistance'.[10] Yet on the other hand, there are concerns that donor assistance can be biased towards the interests of the donor country, or is otherwise poorly tailored to the needs of small developing countries. The challenge for developing countries is to ensure that they use donor support to their advantage, using it to further their interests to the greatest possible extent.

Forms of donor support vary, as do their advantages and disadvantages. The direct provision of consultants is a common form of donor intervention. It is designed to directly increase the number and quality of technically proficient staff available to developing countries. It is common practice among major bilateral donors, such as the EU and United States, to place consultants paid by them in developing country trade ministries and regional organisations, some of whom are given formal roles on the negotiating team of the country. In addition, some donor-financed projects directly fund or subsidise the costs associated with the participation of selected developing countries in negotiations.

---

**Key forms of technical assistance**

*Provision of*

- Consultants to provide technical advice;
- Training workshops for negotiators;
- Financing participation in negotiation meetings;
- Research to inform negotiating positions.

---

A survey of trade negotiators from small developing countries shows that an extremely high number of small states use consultants provided by donors (78 of 80 respondents), with 97 per cent of those whose countries use donor-provided consultants stating they are 'helpful' or 'very helpful' (Jones et al. 2010: 25).

While consultants are clearly perceived to be valuable, negotiators and analysts also raise several concerns. First, there is the risk that excessive reliance on external consultants can undermine, rather than strengthen, the emergence of local expertise and institutional capacity for trade negotiations (Tandon 2004). If external consultants have prepared studies and negotiating positions, negotiators may lack a sense of ownership over the analysis or may consider the quality of work to be deficient, and may not utilise it in the negotiating room.[11] Over time, reliance on external consultants may lead local officials to become disengaged from the negotiating process.

Second, the provision of consultants by donors has been criticised for raising serious conflicts of interest and for posing the risks of breaches of confidentiality. This is most obviously the case if donors have a stake in the outcome of the negotiation. One seasoned negotiator cautioned that developing countries should be on the lookout for 'Trojan horses' in the guise of technical assistance. He cited an instance where an industrialised country offered to 'crunch the numbers' for the Small and Vulnerable Economies coalition to help inform their negotiating position at the WTO. However, when they cross-checked the analysis, the coalition realised that the country concerned was trying to influence their negotiating position in its favour.[12]

Negotiations are most likely to be adversely affected when the country that sits across the negotiating table provides financial assistance. As one experienced analyst notes, 'if a negotiator has his salary paid by a trading partner country, and has travelled to a negotiation with that country on a ticket paid for by that country, it may be difficult for him to disregard this when in the negotiation' (Page 2006).

The provision of training to negotiators is another common form of donor support. Here again, many training and technical assistance initiatives have come under criticism for poor design and delivery of projects and for bias towards supporting the commercial interests of donor countries. A particular concern is that the topics covered in such programmes reflect the negotiating agendas of industrialised rather than developing countries (Tandon 2004). In the words of one negotiator, 'They [large countries] hold workshops and seminars to push their agenda. If people are not very aware, by the time they come to negotiations, they are already half sold' (Jones et al. 2010: 28).

Aside from concerns of bias, negotiators note that the information and analysis provided by external organisations does not always meet the needs of small states. It often fails to reflect the economic realities of their country, tends to be regional rather than country specific and may be based on assumptions about development priorities that are not necessarily shared by the government of the country concerned. As one negotiator commented in the context of the EPA negotiations, 'Most studies are done by NGOs, the EU or outside consultants. Their judgment is influenced by their background. If you have a European background, you may not understand the set-up of an African economy' (Jones et al. 2010: 28).

Importantly, the degree of bias and perceived bias in negotiation-related technical assistance and training varies according to the donor government and the organisation providing support. In many cases, international organisations are perceived as more 'neutral' sources for capacity building than bilateral assistance from developed country governments, not least because they do not sit on the opposite side of the negotiating table.

---

**Steps to ensure assistance benefits the recipient, not the donor**

- **Negotiate for control over how funds are spent** (recruit your own consultants, commission your own studies, determine which experts run training programmes);
- Channel funds through a **neutral intermediary**;
- Ensure the findings and advice of donor-funded assistance are kept **confidential**;
- **Say 'no'** when assistance might be biased or compromising;
- **Do not include external consultants in the negotiating team** or in sensitive preparatory meetings;
- **Staff regional organisations with nationals from the region**, with salaries paid by member states.

---

*What steps can developing countries take to ensure that donor support meets their needs?* Negotiators make two broad recommendations. The first is that developing country governments maintain a high degree of control over consultants and other forms of donor assistance, including through effective oversight and management. This increases the likelihood that support will respond to the country's particular interests and reduces the likelihood that it will be biased towards the interests of donors. For instance, developing country governments might insist that they recruit their own consultants or at least stipulate the criteria on which any consultants are selected; ensure that consultants are accountable solely to them and not the donor organisation; commission their own studies; and determine which experts will run training programmes.

To this end, negotiators may be able to leverage the shift in the donor community towards 'sector-wide approaches', where funds are provided to a ministry based on agreed principles rather than for a specific package of policies or activities. Alternatively, funds can be channelled through a neutral intermediary – a third party that does not have direct interest in the outcome of negotiations. A multi-donor effort also reduces the risks associated with receiving assistance from a single bilateral donor. For instance, the Commonwealth Secretariat manages a multi-donor 'Hub and Spokes' initiative, which provides consultants or 'trade policy analysts' to national governments and regional organisations.

Many negotiators caution against having technical advisers who are directly funded by donors, or who are seconded from donor organisations, on the negotiating team, or in sensitive preparatory meetings. Similarly, they argue that nationals from the region should staff regional organisations and have their salaries paid by member states.

Confidentiality of the reports and advice provided by external consultants is a further area for attention. For instance, the UK government has an explicit policy that the information provided through its assistance projects remains confidential to the recipient government. Similarly, the EU–ACP Project Management Unit insists that all impact assessments that it commissions on behalf of governments of developing countries remain confidential.[13] In general, there is the need for countries to undertake due diligence and examine the reputation and fine print of technical assistance programmes before agreeing to them.

The second recommendation is to 'say no' when assistance is likely to be compromising, or when it is not really needed. A common problem with technical assistance projects is that the default of developing countries is to say 'yes'. Even if there are no concerns of bias, having a plethora of donor-funded projects imposes a cost as precious human resources are spent managing these projects and liaising with donors when they could be invested in initiatives that are more important to the country.

*A common problem with technical assistance projects is that the default of developing countries is to say 'yes'.*

Botswana's experience of negotiating with donors over aid programmes is an interesting example of the ways in which developing countries can ensure that aid works to their advantage (Case Study 29).

---

**Case Study 29: Negotiating with donors: lessons from Botswana**

The government of Botswana has an established strategy for negotiating aid with donors. It uses its domestic planning system to develop a clear agenda and series of projects that are set out in its development plan, and on this basis it approaches donors. It negotiates with individual donors about financing its development efforts, and donors select projects to support from the plan and assess how much to give to the government's total programme through project or programme aid.

Crucially, the government refuses aid that does not fit with its plans and whose recurrent costs cannot be managed. In some cases, it accepts projects initiated by donors, but only after scrutiny and ensuring that it fits with government's priorities and the country's needs. To ensure oversight by government, it insists that projects and project personnel are located and integrated within ministries, resisting the creation of project enclaves. Finally, the government has insisted that donors specialise in sectors to avoid duplication.

The strong planning and coordination of aid by the government has meant that formal donor coordination mechanisms are unnecessary, and the government has resisted the creation of donor coordination mechanism out of concern that they could undermine government priorities.

The factors that help to account for Botswana's success in managing external aid include a relatively low dependence on donor financing, a strong development vision and strong and professional civil service.

*Source*: Whitfield (2009).

## Summary

This chapter has explored the ways in which negotiators can help their countries to address the underlying constraints that impede effective negotiation. This includes advocating for the appropriate level of political attention to be given to trade and closely related policy areas; integrating trade into wider development plans; improving cross-government coordination and communication, including between officials based in capital and those based overseas; and measures to improve recruitment and retention of high-calibre officials. In addition, it has highlighted the need to strengthen the evidence base, both in terms of the collection of reliable data and intelligence, and the quality of policy analysis; strengthen collaboration among countries at the regional level, including through the creation of strong and accountable regional organisations; and use technical assistance to maximum advantage, including 'saying no' when this is appropriate.

---

**Checklist: Putting the Right Foundations in Place**

**Are there clear links between negotiating objectives and the country's wider development strategy?**

**Is the right level of priority accorded to trade negotiations?** If not, how might it be increased?

**What steps can be taken to recruit and retain high-calibre negotiators?**

**How can the quality and relevance of information** available to our negotiators be improved?

**How can cross-government coordination and communication be made more effective?**

Is there sufficient technical and political oversight of regional organisations and regional negotiators?

**What steps can be taken to improve consultation, particularly the quality of inputs from marginal** groups?

Does our trade policy strike the right balance between meeting short-term interests of economic actors and long-term development aspirations?

**Are we getting the most out of technical assistance?** Have we guarded against possible bias?

# 6
# Conclusion

The preceding chapters have shown that negotiators from developing countries manage, in some situations, to manoeuvre deftly and shape outcomes, even when the odds are stacked against them. They have brought together the insights and lessons on how negotiators make this happen, drawing on the best academic research and the experiences of seasoned trade negotiators.

What are the overarching lessons that one might take away from this guide?

## Lesson 1: Invest in preparation

If one lesson stands out, it is the immense value of preparation. Before setting foot into the negotiating arena it is imperative the negotiating team has concrete and precise information of what their government wants from the negotiation, and a deep understanding of the underlying rationale. Developing countries that do well in negotiations invariably have clear and explicit objectives, and their negotiators remain focused on obtaining them.

Yet, if a negotiator is to exert maximum influence during negotiations, preparation needs to go beyond 'knowing what you want'. To excel, negotiators need to have a nuanced understanding of what the other parties at the table are seeking and why. Insights into the particular interests of key government institutions or influential domestic groups, and the personal aspirations of lead negotiators, are particularly precious. Such knowledge helps reveal the competing interests that the other negotiating team will have to manage during the negotiation and is invaluable for identifying 'chinks in their armour' that can be leveraged.

Understanding that the larger country is a collection of interest groups, often in competition with each other, may also make them a less formidable negotiating partner. In the words of one expert, who has advised many small countries on negotiating with the European Union, 'Don't try to negotiate with "the EU". If you do, you are lost. Deal with the interest groups within the EU ....'[1]

During their preparations, negotiators need to build up a nuanced understanding of the power relations in which the negotiations are situated, as this helps determine an appropriate negotiating strategy. Small countries often have sources of leverage and influence that negotiators can draw on, yet they are overlooked. By systematically mapping sources of power, it is possible to identify the tactical moves that will capitalise on these resources to the greatest extent. Having a strong alternative option and a credible threat to walk away is perhaps the most important source of power that a weaker party can have in a negotiation.

Similarly, identifying the sources of power that negotiators from the larger country are likely to draw on, and the tactical moves they are likely to make, enables negotiators to ascertain the best ways to respond. As the saying goes, 'forewarned is forearmed'.

How might the advice to 'prepare well' be put into practice? As one expert argues, it is imperative that negotiators adopt an 'investigative mindset', seeking to find out everything they can about the other party and relevant aspects of the wider political and economic context (Malhotra 2007: 131). Once information is gathered, simulating the negotiations can be a valuable way for ensuring that all the intelligence that has been gathered is used to best effect during the negotiations. The negotiating team from one small developing country, with a reputation for excellence in negotiations, performs role-plays prior to negotiations, and team members simulate the upcoming negotiation as closely as possible. This helps the negotiators analyse and remember the information they have gathered, and enables them to empathise and hence better understand the other party's perspective and to practice making and responding to the tactical moves they are likely to encounter.[2]

## Lesson 2: Use moves away from the table

All too often we think about negotiation as the moments of interaction between parties as they face each other across the negotiating table. Yet, the leading research on negotiations shows that moves made away from the negotiating table exert a decisive influence over outcomes.

Key decisions are made before negotiations formally start, and these influence the manner in which negotiations unfold. All too often, delegations from developing countries arrive at formal negotiations only to find that the set-up is stacked against them: their priority issues are not on the draft agenda, or, worse, they are presented with a template agreement that does not reflect their interests; or the remoteness of the location or timing of the negotiations makes it impractical to field a sufficient number of experts. Paying close attention and exerting influence over seemingly innocuous issues, such as the negotiating agenda, the location where the negotiations can be held or the timing of negotiation rounds, can ensure that negotiators from smaller countries can play to their maximum advantage, or, at the very least, will not be too disadvantaged by the basic set-up.

Paying attention to up-stream discussions can make all the difference when negotiating with a much larger state. Policy processes in large countries often move slowly, and, in the case of more complex trade agreements, it can take years for them to rally all their government departments and domestic stakeholders, and hammer out agreement on a negotiating mandate. The upshot of this protracted internal process is that, once a mandate is agreed and formal negotiations begin, large states are reluctant to make major concessions, as this requires re-opening internal negotiations. In such situations, seeking to influence the very initial internal debates within a large state is likely to yield more success than waiting for formal negotiations to start.

Even when formal negotiations are underway, the guide has highlighted the value that can be gained from making moves away from the negotiating table. Lobbying the political leaders from other states, bringing public opinion onside, working in coalition with other countries and forging alliances with influential stakeholders can help increase the political space available at the negotiating table.

## Lesson 3: Cultivate political skills

International economic negotiations have become incredibly complex and highly technical. For this reason, sophisticated technical skills and an in-depth knowledge of the 'real-world' of economic production and exchange, as well as a formidable grasp of the relevant legal systems are indispensable. It is no wonder that developing countries that are successful in international negotiations invest heavily in ensuring that their negotiators have formidable technical and legal expertise at their disposal.

Yet, this guide suggests that while it is necessary, technical mastery is rarely sufficient for success. It is equally important for a negotiating team to have astute political strategists. Unlike those from large states, negotiators from small states cannot fall back on crude coercive pressure tactics to impose their will – they have to use more subtle forms of power and influence to realise their objectives. It is therefore vital that small developing countries also invest in recruiting, training and retaining deft political operators, and place them at the heart of their negotiating team.

## Lesson 4: Mindset matters

A final overarching lesson is that the mindset with which a negotiator from the smaller party approaches a negotiation can have a decisive influence over the outcome. Many negotiators from small developing countries, quite reasonably, feel overwhelmed at the prospect of negotiating with delegations from countries with far larger economies and more human and financial resources, particularly if their country relies on the other for trade preferences or aid.

Yet, negotiators from small countries that do manage to shape international trade rules see things differently. While realistic about the magnitude of the challenges they face, they are positive that their country can, must and will succeed in its bid to gain from international trade relations. These negotiators are often creative and lateral thinkers, identifying opportunities that others overlook, and they convey a deep sense of purpose, resolve and determination.

Cultivating the right mindset can be an invaluable asset when negotiations become particularly tough. One negotiator explained how, at such moments, he thinks about the people back home whose livelihoods and aspirations are resting on him, and this gives him the resolve to continue.[3] As another negotiator from a very small developing country remarked, 'to succeed in a negotiation, you need to be intellectually, physically, and spiritually prepared'.[4]

## Further reading

While this guide synthesises many of the lessons from the existing literature and studies, readers may wish to examine the issues raised in more depth. Below are some suggestions.

### On negotiating skills

- Malhotra, D. and M. Bazerman (2007). *Negotiation Genius: How to Overcome Obstacles and Achieve Brilliant Results at the Bargaining Table and Beyond.* New York, Bantam Dell.

- Lax, D. and J. Sebenius (2006). *3D Negotiation: Powerful Tools to Change the Game in Your Most Powerful Deals*. Boston, MA, Harvard Business School Press.
- Zartman, I. W. and J. Z. Rubin (2000). *Power and Negotiation*. Ann Arbor, MI, University of Michigan Press.
- Fisher, R. and W. Ury (1991). *Getting to Yes: Negotiating an Agreement without Giving In*. London, Business Books.

## On developing countries in trade negotiations

- Odell, J. (ed.) (2006). *Negotiating Trade: Developing Countries in the WTO and NAFTA*. Cambridge, Cambridge University Press.
- Bhuglah, A. (2004). *A Guide on Trade Negotiations for Small Island Developing States*. New York, UNDP/University of the West Indies.
- Jones, E., C. Deere Birkbeck and N. Woods (2010). *Manoeuvring at the Margins: Constraints Faced by Small States in International Trade Negotiations*. London, Commonwealth Secretariat.

# Notes

## 2  Preparation and Diagnosis

1. Interviews and Focus Group Discussion, July 2011.
2. Workshop with negotiators, London, April 2012.
3. Discussions with negotiators, June 2012.
4. Workshop with negotiators, London, April 2012.

## 3  Moves Away from the Negotiating Table

1. Workshop with negotiators, London, July 2011.
2. Workshop with negotiators, London, April 2012.
3. Workshop with negotiators, London, April 2012.
4. Workshop with negotiators, London, July 2011.
5. Workshop with negotiators, London, July 2011.
6. Decision of Tribunal on Petition from Third Parties to Intervene as Amici Curiae, Methanex Corporation v. United States of America, 15 January 2001, para 49.
7. Interview with key official, September 2008.
8. Workshop with negotiators, London, April 2012.

## 4  Moves at the Negotiating Table

1. Workshop with negotiators, London, April 2012.
2. Workshop with arbitrators, University of Oxford, June 2012.
3. Workshop with negotiators, London, April 2012.
4. See, for instance, Industry Trade Advisory Committee on Intellectual Property Rights (ITAC-15) (2006). *The U.S.-Peru Trade Promotion Agreement (TPA): The Intellectual Property Provisions*. Washington DC, Industry Trade Advisory Committee on Intellectual Property Rights (ITAC-15).

## 5  Putting the Right Foundations in Place

1. See www.moti.gov.gh.
2. Workshops with trade negotiators, London, July 2011 and April 2012.
3. Workshops with trade negotiators, London, July 2011 and April 2012.
4. Workshop with negotiators, London, April 2012.
5. See www.iisd.org/investment/capacity/.
6. Workshop with negotiators, London, April 2012.
7. Workshop with negotiators, London, April 2012.
8. Workshop with negotiators, London, April 2012.

9. Workshop with trade negotiators, London, July 2011.
10. Workshop with negotiators, London, April 2012.
11. Workshop with negotiators, London, April 2012.
12. Interview with trade negotiator, September 2008.
13. Workshop with negotiators, London, April 2012.

## 6  Conclusion

1. Interview with a policy adviser to small developing countries, August 2008.
2. Discussion with small state negotiator, April 2012.
3. Interview with trade negotiator, July 2008.
4. Discussion with trade negotiator, January 2010.

# References

Alba V. C. and G. C. Vega (2002). Trade Advisory Mechanisms in Mexico. In *The Trade Policy-Making Process Level One of the Two Level Game: Country Studies in the Western Hemisphere*. Ed. S. Ostry, P. Hakim and J. J. Taccone. Argentina, INTAL-ITD-STA.

Alschner, W. (2011). Interpretation of International Investment Agreements: What states can do. *IIA Issue Note*. Geneva, Switzerland, UNCTAD.

Bhattacharya, D. et al. (2004). The EU-EBA Initiative: Market Access Implications and Potential Benefits for Bangladesh. *Occasional Paper*. Dhaka, Bangladesh, Centre for Policy Dialogue.

Bhuglah, A. (2004). *A Handbook on Trade Negotiations for Small Island Developing States*. UNDP/University of the West Indies.

Bilal, S. et al. (2007). Talking Trade: Practical Insights on the Capacity to Conduct trade Negotiations. In *Navigating New Waters: A Reader on EU-ACP Trade Relations Vol.2*. Ed. S. Bilal and R. Grynberg. London, Commonwealth Secretariat. pp. 310–328.

Bounds, A. (2007). Islands Threaten to Halt EU Trade Talks. *Financial Times*. Brussels. [August 2nd].

Breckenridge, J. (2005). Costa Rica's Challenge to US Restrictions on the Import of Underwear. In *Managing the Challenges of WTO Participation – 45 Case Studies*. Ed. P. Gallagher, P. Low and A. L. Stoler. Geneva, WTO. pp. 178–188.

Carrion, G. (2009). Trade, Regionalism and the Politics of Policy Making in Nicaragua. *Markets, Business and Regulation Programme Paper*. Geneva, UNRISD.

Cato, J. C. and S. Subasinge (2003). Food Safety in Food Security and Food Trade, Case Study: The Shrimp Export Industry in Bangladesh. *Brief 9 of 17, Focus 10*. Washington DC, IFPRI.

Davis, C. L. (2006). Do WTO Rules Create a Level Playing Field? Lessons from Peru and Vietnam. In *Negotiating Trade: Developing Countries in the WTO and NAFTA*. Ed. J. Odell. Cambridge, Cambridge University Press, pp. 219–256.

Deere, C. (2005). International Trade technical Assistance and Capacity Building. *Human Development Report Occasional Paper*. New York, UNDP.

Deere Birkbeck, C. (2009). *The Implementation Game: The TRIPS Agreement and the Global Politics of Intellectual Property Reform in Developing Countries*. Oxford, Oxford University Press.

Deere Birkbeck, C. (2011). Development-oriented Agendas for Global Trade Governance: A Summary of Proposals. In *Making Global Trade Governance Work for Development: Perspectives and Priorities from Developing Countries*. Ed. C. Deere Birkbeck. Cambridge, Cambridge University Press. pp. 579–667.

Deere Birkbeck, C. and M. Harbourd (2011). Developing Country Coalitions in the WTO: Strategies for Improving the Influence of the WTO's Weakest and Poorest Members. *GEG Working Paper*. Oxford, Global Economic Governance Programme.

Devereaux, C. et al. (2006a). Brazil's WTO Cotton Case: Negotiation Through Litigation. In *Case Studies in US Trade Negotiation: Resolving Disputes*. Ed. Charan Devereaux, R. Z. Lawrence and M. D. Watkins. Washington, DC, Institute for International Economics. pp. 235–282.

Devereaux, C. et al. (2006b). Case Studies in US Trade Negotiation: Making the Rules. Institute for International Economics, Washington, DC.

Dunlop, A. et al. (2004). Organising Trade Negotiating Capacity at Regional Level: A Caribbean Case Study. *Discussion Paper*. Maastrict, Belgium, ECPDM.

Eagleton-Pierce, M. D. (2012). The Competing Kings of Cotton: (Re)framing the WTO African Cotton Initiative. *New Political Economy*, Vol. 17, Issue 3, pp. 313–337.

Echandi, R. (2006). The DR-CAFTA-US FTA Negotiations in Financial Services: The Experience of Costa Rica, *Paper prepared for the World Bank*.

Fattouh, B. and H. Darbouche (2010). North African Oil and Foreign Investment in Changing Market Conditions. *Energy Policy* 38(2): 1119–1129.

Fisher, R. and W. Ury (1991). *Getting to Yes: Negotiating an Agreement without Giving In*. London, Business Books.

Garay, L. G. et al. (2011). Negotaiting the Colombia-US FTA: A Colombian Perspective. In *Asymmetric Trade Negotaitions*. Ed. S. Bilal, P. De Lombaerde and D. Tussie. Surrey, UK, Ashgate. pp. 137–166.

Goodison, P. (2010). EU Trade Negotiations: Structures, Processes, Policy Perspectives and Negotiating Approaches. *Paper for the Commonwealth Secretariat*.

Gray Molina, G. (2010). Global Governance Exit: A Bolivian Case Study. Paper was prepared for the 2nd Annual GLF Colloquium, 3–4 May 2010.

Gruber, L. (2001). Power Politics and the Free Trade Bandwagon. *Comparative Political Studies* 34(7): 703.

Guimarães de Lima e Silva, V. r. (2012). International Regime Complexity and Enhanced Enforcement of Intellectual Property Rights: The Use of Networks at the Multilateral Level. *GEG Working Paper*. Oxford, UK, Global Economic Governance Programme, University of Oxford.

Haider, M. Z. (2007). Competitiveness of the Bangladesh Ready-made Garment Industry in Major International Markets. *Asia-Pacific Trade and Investment Review* 3(1): 3–27.

Haroon, J. U. (2011). Bangladesh Textiles Hit By New EU Trade Rules. *Financial Express*, Dhaka, Bangladesh.

Harun, Y. A. (2010). Regional Cooperation in South Asia: Bangladesh Perspective. In *Promoting Economic Cooperation in South Asia: Beyond SAFTA*. Ed. S. Ahmed, S. Kelegama and E. Ghani. Washington, DC, USA IBRD/World Bank. pp. 279–299.

Harvard Business Essentials (2005). *Power, Influence, and Persuasion: Sell Your Ideas and Make Things Happen: Sell Your Idea and Make Things Happen*. Boston, MA, Harvard Business Schools Press.

HBSP (2005). *The Essentials of Negotiation*. Boston, Harvard Business School Press (HBSP).

Heinisch, E. L. (2006). "West Africa Versus the United States on Cotton Subsidies: How, Why and What Next?" *The Journal of Modern African Studies* 44(02): 251–274.

Hicks, R. et al. (forthcoming). Trade Policy, Economic Interests and Party Politics in a Developing Country: The Political Economy of CAFTA. *International Studies Quarterly*. Massachusetts, USA, Harvard University.

Hirschman, A. O. (1945). *National Power and the Structure of Foreign Trade*. Berkeley and Los Angeles, University of California press.

Hussain, T. (2005). Victory in Principle: Pakistan's Dispute Settlement Case on Combed Cotton Yarn Exports to the United States. In *Managing the Challenges of WTO Participation: 45 Case Studies*. Ed. P. Gallagher, P. Low and A. L. Stoler. Cambridge, UK, Cambridge University Press. pp. 459–472.

ICTSD (2010). US, Brazil Agree to Negotiate End to Cotton Dispute. *Bridges Weekly Trade News Digest* Vol 14, Number 13, 14th April 2010, Geneva.

Industry Trade Advisory Committee on Intellectual Property Rights (ITAC-15) (2006). *The U.S.-Peru Trade Promotion Agreement (TPA): The Intellectual Property Provisions*. Washington DC, Industry Trade Advisory Committee on Intellectual Property Rights (ITAC-15).

Insanally, R. (2011). The Sugar Lobby 2004–6: A Case for More Innovative Diplomacy. In *CARICOM: Options for International Engagement*. Ed. K. O. Hall and M. Chuck-a-Sang. London, UK, Commonwealth Secretariat. pp. 308–331.

Jones, E. et al. (2010). *Manoeuvring at the Margins: Constraints Faced by Small States in International Trade Negotiations*. London, Commonwealth Secretariat.

Julian, M. et al. (2007). EPA Negotiations Update. *Trade Negotiations Insights 7*, Geneva, Switzerland, ICTSD.

Lang, O. (2009). Maldives Leader in Climate Change Stunt. *BBC News (Online)*, London, UK, BBC.

Lattimer, M. (2000). *The Campaigning Handbook*. London, Directory of Social Change.

Laurent, E. (2006). Understanding International Trade: The Trading System From the Perspective of the Eastern Caribbean. Castries, St Lucia, OCES Trade Policy Project.

Laurent, E. (2007). Small States in the Banana Dispute and the Lessons to be Learned from their Experience. In *Navigating New Waters: A Reader on ACP-EU Trade Relations*, vol. 1. Ed. S. Bilal and R. Grynberg. London, Commonwealth Secretariat. pp. 440–453.

Lax, D. and J. Sebenius (2004) Negotiation: the right set-up makes a deal. *Financial Times*. Brussels. [August 3rd] [newspaper article].

Lax, D. and J. Sebenius (2006). *3D Negotiation: Powerful Tools to Change the Game in Your Most Powerful Deals*. Boston, MA, Harvard Business School Press.

Mahler, V. A. (1981). "Britain, the European Community, and the Developing Commonwealth: Dependence, Interdependence, and the Political Economy of Sugar. *International Organization* 35(3): 467–492.

Malhotra, D. and M. H. Bazerman (2007). *Negotiation Genius: How to Overcome Obstacles and Achieve Brilliant Results at the Bargaining Table and Beyond*. New York, Bantam Books.

Mkandawire, T. (2010). From Maladjusted States to Democratic Developmental States in Africa. In *Constructing a Democratic Developmental State in South Africa*. Ed. Omano Edigheji Cape Town, South Africa, HSRC Press. pp. 59–81.

Mo, J. (2004). Democratic Consolidation and Multilateral Trade Negotiation Strategies: Korean Negotiators at the Uruguay Round. In *How to Negotiate Over Trade: A Summary of New Research for Developing Countries*. Ed. J. S. Odell and A. Ortiz Mena. Geneva, Geneva International Academic Network. pp. 11–12.

Moon, S. (2011). Meaningful Technology Transfer to the LDCs: A Proposal for a Monitoring Mechanism for TRIPS Article 66.2. *Policy Brief 9 (April 2011)*. Geneva, ICTSD.

Narlikar, A. (2003). *International Trade and Developing Countries: Bargaining and Coalitions in the GATT and WTO*. London; New York, Routledge.

Narlikar, A. (2006). Fairness in International Trade Negotiations: Developing Countries in the GATT and WTO. *World Economy* 29(8): 1005–1029.

Narlikar, A. and J. Odell (2006). The Strict Distributive Strategy for a Bargaining Colaition: the Like-Minded Group in the World Trade Organisation. In *Negotiating Trade: Developing Countries in the WTO and NAFTA*. Ed. J. Odell. Cambridge, UK, Cambridge University Press. pp. 115–144.

Nye, J. S. (2010). The Pros and Cons of Citizen Diplomacy. *New York Times*. New York, USA.

Odell, J. (1999). The Negotiation Process and International Economic Organizations. Paper prepared for delivery at the 1999 Annual Meeting of the American Political Science Association, Atlanta Marriott Marquis and Atlanta Hilton and Towers, September 2–5, 1999, University of Southern California. [available at: www-bcf.usc.edu/~odell/APSA99.DOC].

Odell, J. and B. Eichengreen (1998). The United States, the ITO, and the WTO: Exit Options, Agent Slack, and Presidential Leadership. In *The WTO as an International Organization*. Ed. A. O. Krueger. Chicago, University of Chicago Press. pp. 181–209.

Odell, J. and A. Ortiz Mena (2004). *How to Negotiate Over Trade: A Summary of New Research for Developing Countries*. Geneva, Geneva International Academic Network.

Odell, J. S. (1985). The Outcomes of International Trade Conflicts: The US and South Korea, 1960–1981. *International Studies Quarterly* 29(3): 263–286.

Odell, J. S. (2000). *Negotiating the World Economy*. Ithaca, NY/London, Cornell University Press.

Odell, J. S. (2006) Introduction. In *Negotiating Trade: Developing Countries in the WTO and NAFTA*. Ed. J. Odell. Cambridge, Cambridge University Press. pp. 1–40.

Odell (2010) Negotiating from Weakness in International Trade Relations, *Journal of World Trade* 44(2010): 545–566.

Odell, J. S. and S. Sell (2006). Reframing the Issue: The WTO Coalition on Intellectual Property and Public Health, 2001. In *Negotiating Trade: Developing Countries in the WTO and NAFTA*. Ed. J. Odell. Cambridge, Cambridge University Press. pp. 85–114.

Ortiz Mena, A. (2006). Getting to 'No': Defending Against Demands in NAFTA Energy Negotiations. In *Negotiating Trade: Developing Countries in the WTO and NAFTA*. Ed. J. Odell. Cambridge, Cambridge University Press. pp. 177–218.

Ostry, J. D. et al. (2011). Managing Capital Inflows: What Tools to Use? *IMF Staff Discussion Note*, IMF.

Page, S. (2006). Bringing Aid and Trade Together. In *Trade and Aid: Rivals or Partners in Development Policy?* Ed. S. Page. London, Cameron May. pp. 11–34.

Page, S. (2011). Better Regulations and Better Negotiations as Tools for Trade: Where Aid for Trade Can and Cannot Help. Presented at OECD Experts Workshop on Aid for Trade Implementation 29 March 2011, ODI.

Panke, D. (2011). Microstates in Negotiations beyond the Nation-State: Malta, Cyprus and Luxembourg as Active and Successful Policy Shapers? *International Negotiation* 16(2): pp. 297–317.

Patel, M. (2011). *Mobilising in the Periphery: African Coalition Bargaining in the WTO.* DPhil thesis, University of Oxford.

Polaski, S. (2006). *Winners and Losers: Impact of the Doha Round on Developing Countries.* Washington DC, Carnegie Endowment for International Peace.

Program on Negotiation at Harvard Law School (2009). Coping with Culture at the Bargaining Table. *Negotiation Journal,* 12(7): July 2009.

Pupphavesa, W. et al. (2011). Negotiating the Thailand-US Free Trade Agreement. In *Asymmetric Trade Negotiations.* Ed. S. Bilal, P. De Lombaerde and D. Tussie. Surrey, UK, Ashgate. pp. 167–180.

Rahman, M. (2002). Market Access Implications of SPS and TBT: Bangladesh Perspective. *Research Report.* Jaipur, India, CUTS Centre for International Trade, Economics and Environment.

Rodrik, D. (2001). *The Global Governance of Trade as if Development Really Mattered: Report Submitted to UNDP.* Cambridge, MA, Harvard University.

Salacuse, J. W. (2000). Lessons for Practice. In *Power and Negotiation.* Ed. I. W. Zartman and J. Z. Rubin. Ann Arbor, University of Michigan Press. pp. 255–270.

Sánchez-Ancochea, D. (2008). State and Society: The Political Economy of DR-CAFTA in Costa Rica, the Dominican Republic and El Salvador. In *Responding to Globalization: The Political Economy of Hemispheric Integration in the Americas.* Ed. D. Sánchez-Ancochea and K. Shadlen. Basingstoke, Palgrave MacMillan. pp. 171–200.

Sebenius, J. (1984). *Negotiating the Law of the Sea: Lessons in the Art and Science of Reaching Agreement* Cambridge, MA, Harvard University Press.

Singh, J. P. (2006). The Evolution of National Interests: New Issues and North–South Negotiations during the Uruguay Round. In *Negotiating Trade: Developing Countries in the WTO and NAFTA.* Ed. J. Odell. Cambridge, Cambridge University Press. pp. 41–85.

Subramanian, A. (2009). The Mauritian Success Story and its Lessons. *Research Paper.* Helsinki, Finland, UNU-WIDER.

Tandon, Y. (2004). Technical Assistance as a Policy Instrument. In *The Reality of Trade: The WTO and Developing Countries.* Ed. Chantal Blouin Ottawa, Canada, North-South Institute. pp. 62–74.

Thompson, L. L. (2012). *The Mind and Heart of the Negotiator.* Upper Saddle River, NJ, Prentice Hall.

Tienhaara, K. S. (2008). The Expropriation of Environmental Governance: Protecting Foreign Investors at the Expense of Public Policy. *PhD Thesis.* Amsterdam, Vrije Universiteit Amsterdam.

Trotz, U. (2011). The Caribbean and Climate Change Negotiations In Copenhagen, December 2009. In *CARICOM: Options for International Engagement.* Ed. K. O. Hall and M. Chuck-a-Sang. London, UK, Commonwealth Secretariat. pp. 421–426.

Tussie, D. and M. Saguier (2011). The Sweep of Asymmetric Trade Negotiations: Introduction and Overview. In *Asymmetric Trade Negotiations.* Ed. S. Bilal, P. De Lombaerde and D. Tussie. Surry, UK, Ashgate. pp. 1–26.

UNCTAD (2011). Scope and Definition: UNCTAD Series on Issues in International Investment Agreements II.

Whitfield, L. (2009). *The Politics of Aid: African Strategies for Dealing with Donors.* Oxford/New York, Oxford University Press.

Woolcock, S. (2010). The Treaty of Lisbon and the European Union as an actor in international trade. Working Paper ECIPE.

Xuto, N. (2005). Thailand: Conciliating a Dispute on Tuna Exports to the EC. In *Managing the Challenges of WTO Participation: 45 Case Studies*. Ed. P. Gallagher, P. Low and A. L. Stoler. Cambridge, Cambridge University Press. pp. 555–565.

Zafar, A. (2012). Mauritius: An Economic Success Story. In *Yes Africa Can: Success Stories from a Dynamic Continent*. Ed. P. Chuhan-Pole and M. Angwafo. Washington, DC, The World Bank. pp. 91–106.

Zartman, I. W. and J. Z. Rubin (2000). Symmetry and Asymmetry in Negotiation. In *Power and Negotiation*. Ed. I. W. zartman and J. Z. Rubin. Ann Arbor, University of Michigan Press. pp. 271–293.

# Index

Printed and bound in Great Britain by
CPI Antony Rowe, Chippenham and Eastbourne